November 22, 2019

To Barb –

A guide to discipleship that we are going thru! Hope it inspires you!

Love – Toni.

D1476404

WORDS OF GRATITUDE

The authors wish to express their gratitude to:

JoAnn Buckman for her exceptional layout and graphic design skills. She brought visual life and space to all of our thoughts.

Michelle Koenig for her leadership and advanced skills in the editing and proofreading process and the countless times she read and re-read the Discipleship Guide to help get it to the place it is today.

Kim Link, Nicole Murray and Amanda Davies for proofreading and editing. They went through the exhausting and tedious task of fixing our mistakes and creating consistency.

Courtney Smith for her technical skills in getting the Discipleship Assessment online. We are so excited to see how this will shine a light on our areas of strengths and weaknesses in our discipleship journey.

Our discipleship groups who tested the guide and provided practical and in-depth feedback:
Radiant: Kay's group
Young Adults: Adam's group
Friends and Allies of Jesus: Doug's group

Bob Krulish for his extensive wisdom on discipleship.

Jasona Brown who wrote Appendices C, H and I - giving us tremendous insight into discipleship, barriers to growth and healing prayer.

Greenwood Elders for their invaluable input into the discipleship process.

The Greenwood Congregation whom we love and are humbled to serve.

Our wonderful spouses, David Morrison, Angie Long and Jasona Brown, who have been God's greatest gift to our own spiritual formation.

And lastly, but most importantly, we are grateful to Jesus and His continual invitation for us.

THE INVITATIONS OF JESUS

A DISCIPLESHIP GUIDE

BY KAY MORRISON, ADAM LONG AND DOUG BROWN

CONTENTS

• —•— •

INTRODUCTION

Introduction to the Discipleship Guide . . . 8

Stories of the Authors . . . 10

OPENING CONCEPTS

—• Session 1 . . . 14
What is a Disciple?

—• Session 2 . . . 17
Foundational Truths and Five Phases of Spiritual Growth

—• Session 3 . . . 23
Starting Point: Good News!

THE INVITATIONS OF JESUS

—• INTRODUCTION . . . *28*

—• WORSHIP & PRAYER
Come . . . *32*
Know . . . *36*
Breathe . . . *41*

—• COMMUNITY
Together . . . *48*
Conversation . . . *53*
Rest . . . *57*

—• MISSION
Serve . . . *64*
Give . . . *67*
Go . . . *73*

CONTENTS

APPENDICES

A. Lectio Divina . . . 78

B. Sanctification Diagram . . . 80

C. Barriers to Intimacy with God . . . 81

D. Bible Study Basics and Three Stages of Inductive Bible Study . . . 83

E. A Contemplative Lord's Prayer . . . 88

F. Identity for Those in Christ . . . 89

G. Attributes of God . . . 91

H. The Immanuel Moment . . . 94

I.   The Role of Healing Prayer in Discipleship . . . 96

J. Prayer, Care and Share . . . 98

K. The Remaining Task of Missions . . . 101

Leader's Guide . . . 104

Recommended Reading List of the Authors . . . 107

INTRODUCTION

*Introduction to the Discipleship Guide
and Stories of the Authors*

INTRODUCTION

. . . .

Have you ever wondered if there is more to life? Does your heart ever ache for more than seems offered in a culture obsessed with self? Could there be more meaning, more joy, more love, more peace, more kindness, more healing, more hope?

We believe there is more.

We believe there is so much more to life, because Jesus offers us more - a quality of life beyond the ordinary. The very best life there is - the life God created us to live. Jesus offers us LIFE with Him in God's beautiful Kingdom (John 10:10).

We desire for you to experience LIFE with Jesus, because there's more!

There is more to following Jesus than saying yes to Him and then slugging through life waiting for heaven. There is more to following Jesus than a transaction with God to avoid the "bad place" and get into the "good place." There is more to following Jesus than just going to church on Sundays. There is more to following Jesus than living a life of safety, comfort and pleasure doing whatever you think is right.

Jesus invites us to follow Him in a life-long, life-giving, joyful relationship as His disciple. We experience LIFE with Jesus in God's beautiful Kingdom now as we wholeheartedly live as His disciples. As His disciples, we embrace God's Story as the story of the world that gives us our truest identity, value and purpose.

Wherever we are, Jesus invites each of us into more. His desire for us is to come to Him and follow Him as King of our lives. Jesus invites us to know Him fully and to know ourselves as He knows us, to live surrendered and empowered by His Spirit and in loving union with Him.

Jesus models and teaches a way of living attentively to God's Presence and priorities. His way is expressed in the rhythms of worship and prayer, community and mission (Mark 3:13-15, Luke 6:12-19).

Jesus invites us to live in continuous conversation with Him and as part of a community of faith where we can be known and loved. He longs for us to rest in Him and live from a place of rest, free from striving.

Jesus invites us to live like Him and give our lives away: serving and loving Him and those around us; opening our hands to Him with all we have; and living on mission with Him in obedience to the Great Commission and Great Command to see His Kingdom come, breaking through our lost and broken world with His gospel of grace and making disciples of Jesus through us.

If you desire to say yes to His invitations and live the life of a disciple, then gather with a few friends and use this guide as you journey together. At the beginning of this guide, you'll find some information that is foundational to the journey of a disciple. Your group can begin by discussing the Opening Concepts and then taking the Discipleship Assessment (see page 20).

Following the Opening Concepts are Nine Invitations of Jesus. Each of the invitations includes a story; a guided Bible study; practices to engage your head, heart and hands; spiritual exercises; Lectio Divina; and a verse to memorize. You can devote a week or more to each invitation. You will find supplemental appendices, a list of books recommended by the authors and a Leader's Guide at the back of this guide.

We are praying that as you journey together with fellow friends of Jesus, you will be blessed by this guide.

May the God Who loves you, called you to Himself and made you alive, meet and transform you as you walk with Him through this guide. May you discover the beauty and joy of being a disciple of King Jesus. And may His grace empower you to live as His disciple all the days of your life, now and forever. Amen.

OUR STORIES

. . . .

——• KAY MORRISON

As far back as I can remember, I knew who Jesus was. I gave my life to Him as a middle school girl and experienced slow growth in my faith in the next few years. But my relationship with Jesus changed while I was in college. As a 19-year-old sophomore, I met Charmaine during sorority rush. As our friendship grew, I saw that Charmaine's faith was different than mine - vibrant, joyful, full of love and intimacy with Jesus. I wanted that. I began reading through the gospel of John and asking the Spirit to show me more and He did. As I laid in bed each night reading by a flashlight, the words on the pages were alive, pulsing with excitement and opportunity. Within days, two friends invited me to be in a discipleship Bible study. We met each Thursday night, studied the Word, prayed together and shared our hearts and lives. These relationships were where God first met me with the life-changing reality of growing as His disciple.

> **As I laid in bed each night reading by a flashlight, the words on the pages were alive, pulsing with excitement and opportunity.**

A few years later in my life, I was stuck facing a significant struggle and in futility trying to address it on my own. Graciously, the Lord led me to Iris, an older, wiser woman. Iris loved Jesus and was devoted to Him and His call to disciple others. Through her wisdom, powerful prayers and almost daily investment in discipling me, I experienced God's grace changing me and setting me free. Because of this experience, I have sought to follow Jesus by discipling younger women, many in this same struggle. It is a sacred privilege to watch and partner with the Holy Spirit as He transforms lives.

It is through these and many other life-altering relationships that my faith has been strengthened by the Spirit and threaded all the way through by His powerful, transforming grace.

⟶ ADAM LONG

If someone were to ask me, "What has made the greatest impact in your life?" I would obviously say, "God!" But more specifically, God through people discipling me - people intentionally walking alongside me, showing me the ways of Jesus and His heart for others and the world.

First off it was my parents, Ben and Joyce. Now as a parent of two boys, I am so much more aware of how my parents planted seeds of God's Word in my life; reflected the love and grace of Jesus; discipled many through an open life and home; faithfully served as missionaries in Singapore; and impacted spiritual generations. I find myself even using the phrases they would often say. They laid the foundation in my life so when I headed off to college and struggled with anxiety and depression, those seeds came to life as my own faith was sustained by His grace and power.

> **... when I headed off to college and struggled with anxiety and depression, those seeds came to life as my own faith was sustained by His grace and power.**

While in college I had two men who intentionally discipled me, Ron and Kevin. Ron taught me how to study and memorize the Bible, disciple and witness to others and helped open my heart for missions as we served together in Vilnius, Lithuania for two summers. Kevin was like a spiritual shepherd who saw me with all my complexities and affirmed my pursuit of engineering and my heart for missions. We would often discuss the depths of theology together and with his beer-drinking, pipe-smoking ways, he burst my conservative Christian bubble of what a follower of Jesus looked like. He showed me an integrated soul that was incarnationally living out his faith in every context.

These mentors, and many more, set the trajectory of my life and gave me a passion for discipling others.

⟶• DOUG BROWN

Shortly after surrendering my life to Jesus Christ as a young lawyer, Mark invited me to be a part of a small group of men seeking to grow as disciples of Jesus. These men lived ordinary lives, and they honestly wanted to grow as Jesus' disciples as husbands, fathers and businessmen. That experience, meeting weekly for two years, was like spiritual "Miracle Grow." It wasn't just the Bible study or Christian classics we read, but the shared life together. I was able to learn as much from the way I saw them living their lives as I did from God's Word. Those peer relationships, under the leadership of our more mature leader, launched me into a life-long journey of following Jesus.

"

This basic practice, commanded by our Lord and rooted in His community, is the great need of our time.

"

I am forever thankful and indebted to the men and women who have walked alongside me to help me follow Jesus Christ as my Lord and Savior. Drew encouraged me to remain faithful in singleness while I longed to be married. Toni and others introduced me to the healing presence of Jesus. Dr. Waltke and Dr. Fee imparted to me a passion for good theology. My wife, Jasona, is more than my beloved covenant partner. She is my ally with Jesus for His glory and Kingdom.

Without their prayers, counsel, teaching and encouragement, my life would look significantly different. I am sure I would not have experienced the joy, intimacy and freedom in the Lord that I have without these faithful men and women doing what Jesus calls all of us to do - disciple others. This basic practice, commanded by our Lord and rooted in His community, is the great need of our time.

OPENING CONCEPTS

Session 1
What is a Disciple?

Session 2
Foundational Truths and Five Phases of Spiritual Growth

Session 3
Starting Point: Good News!

SESSION 1
What is a Disciple?

....

A disciple is an apprentice, a learner, a follower. The Greek word *mathētés* means a 'disciple' or 'learner' or 'pupil'. The word disciple has two aspects to it: the relationship of a student to a teacher, and the notion of following along behind someone. First and foremost, our discipleship is to Jesus, our relationship with Him and following Him (Matthew 16:24-25). A disciple of Jesus is one who has received new life through the Spirit and whose life now comes under the authority and rule of King Jesus.

"At its simplest Christ's call was "Follow me." He asked men and women for their personal allegiance. He invited them to learn from him, to obey his words and to identify themselves with his cause." - John Stott

⎯⎯• WHAT IS DISCIPLESHIP?

"Discipling is a relationship where we intentionally walk alongside a growing disciple or disciples in order to encourage, correct, and challenge them to grow toward maturity in Christ." - Greg Ogden

For a follower of Jesus, discipleship (also called sanctification, spiritual growth or spiritual formation) is the dynamic, relational, life-long process of grace that restores us to God's original intent for our lives and transforms us into the likeness of Jesus. A disciple of Jesus is one who has received new life through the Spirit and whose life now comes under the authority and rule of King Jesus.

Discipleship is the work of grace through the power of the Holy Spirit and the participation of the believer. Discipleship requires our willingness and intention to follow Jesus. It is an inward work with external evidence. As the Spirit begins to change our hearts, our thoughts and desires become more like Jesus and then our motivations and actions change too.

"Disciples are those who, seriously intending to become like Jesus from the inside out, systematically and progressively rearrange their affairs to that end, under the guidance of the Word and the Spirit." - Dallas Willard

Discipleship occurs as hearts are regenerated, enabling a disciple to love God and others.

 *"And I will give you a **new heart**, and I will put a new spirit in you. I will take out your stony, stubborn heart and give you **a tender, responsive heart**." Ezekiel 36:26*

 *"Jesus replied, '**You must love the Lord your God with all your heart, all your soul, and all your mind**.'" Matthew 22:37*

Discipleship is ultimately a work of the heart as people willingly and actively embrace biblical truth and grow in love for Jesus in the context of community, which results in progressively changed lives that look more and more like Jesus.

Discipleship is about multiplication. Disciples are those who make disciples who make disciples. It started with God's call to Adam and Eve "to be fruitful and multiply" (Genesis 1:28), and Jesus continues the call to multiply in the Great Commission to "make disciples of all nations" (Matthew 28:19). This was not a command merely to the apostles, but a command to us that has echoed through the history of the church.

Love for God deepens, love for His people grows and love compels a disciple to make disciples, reach out to the lost and to live on mission for the Kingdom of Jesus.

"For above all else, the Christian life is a love affair of the heart. It cannot be lived primarily as a set of principles or ethics. It cannot be managed with steps and programs. It cannot be lived exclusively as a moral code leading to righteousness. ... The truth of the gospel is intended to free us to love God and others with a whole heart." - Brent Curtis and John Eldredge

———• LECTIO DIVINA

Luke 5:1-11 (See Appendix A for guidance on Lectio Divina.)

———• DISCUSSION QUESTIONS

1. How do these thoughts on discipleship differ from your previous understanding?

2. Does the quote from Brent Curtis and John Eldredge, "*the Christian life is a love affair of the heart*," resonate with you? Has this been your experience?

3. What is your hope for your journey as a disciple? Is there a clear next step for you? Ask the Lord to give you the grace needed.

SESSION 2
Foundational Truths

. . . .

These five truths are critical to understanding the discipleship process.

1. **Discipleship is not linear.** It is not a formulaic, smooth, linear movement (see Appendix B). Often we feel like we are going backward when we're actually growing! True discipleship is messy.

   ———

   "Following Christ is anything but tidy and neat, balanced and orderly. Far from it. Spirituality is complex, complicated and perplexing - the disorderly, sloppy, chaotic look of authentic faith in the real world. Spirituality is anything but a straight line; it is a mixed-up, topsy-turvy, helter-skelter godliness that turns our lives into an upside-down toboggan ride full of unexpected turns, surprise bumps, and bone-shattering crashes. In other words, messy spirituality is the delirious consequence of a life ruined by a Jesus who will love us right into His arms." - Mike Yaconelli

   ———

2. **Discipleship is relational.** The heart of salvation is relational - through faith in Jesus, our relationship with God is restored. Sanctification is a relational process with God and with His people. God reorients our hearts to **worship** Him; to live in a new **community**, the family of God; and to be on **mission** to the lost. Therefore, disciples need to be worshipping in a local church where they are known and have a small community of believers participating in their lives.

   Growth takes place in Christ-centered community, where the "one anothers" of Scripture are lived out and His love is expressed outwardly to those who don't know Him. With intentionality, a disciple follows the biblical model of relationship, both being discipled and discipling others.

   Discipleship involves asking two relational questions of the Word, the Spirit and one another:

   What is God saying?
   How do I respond?

"How can I ever let God's grace fully work in my life unless I live in a community of people who can affirm it, deepen it, and strengthen it? We cannot live this new life alone. God does not want to isolate us by his grace. On the contrary, he wants us to form new friendships and a new community - holy places where his grace can grow to fullness and bear fruit." - Henri Nouwen

"To be truly biblical, as well as truly effective, the growth process must include the Body of Christ." - Dr. Henry Cloud and Dr. John Townsend

3. **Discipleship is a work of the Holy Spirit.** Willingness to surrender to the Holy Spirit and obey Him is a prerequisite to growth. It takes effort on the part of the disciple. We usually grow as much as we're willing to grow.

"The path of spiritual growth in the riches of Christ is not a passive one. Grace is not opposed to effort. It is opposed to earning. Effort is action. Earning is attitude. You have never seen people more active than those who have been set on fire by the grace of God. Paul, who perhaps understood grace better than any other mere human being, looked back at what had happened to him and said: "By the grace of God I am what I am, and his grace toward me did not prove vain; but I labored even more than all of them, yet not I, but the grace of God with me." (I Corinthians: 15:10) - Dallas Willard

4. **Discipleship involves adversity and suffering.** We shouldn't be surprised that God uses suffering and hardships of all kinds to produce growth. Jesus told us we would suffer. But God in His grace and mercy takes our suffering and uses it for our benefit and blessing. Some of the greatest strides in growth occur in seasons of difficulty.

 "Consider it pure joy, my brothers and sisters, whenever you face trials of many kinds, because you know that the testing of your faith produces perseverance. Let perseverance finish its work so that you may be mature and complete, not lacking anything." James 1:2-3

In addition to suffering for righteousness and the name of Jesus, God's Word indicates that we all struggle and suffer with a certain measure of frailty or weakness simply because we live in a broken world (Romans 8:18-27). God has compassion on us as we struggle with our frailty, weaknesses and limitations (Psalm 103:13-14). Jesus promises us that these weaknesses can even become the very places where we experience His grace and power more intimately. Jesus uses our frailty and weakness to grow us in our dependence on Him (2 Corinthians 12:7-10).

"'But he said to me, 'My grace is sufficient for you, for my power is made perfect in weakness.' Therefore, I will boast more gladly about my weaknesses, so that Christ's power may rest on me. That's why for Christ's sake, I delight in weaknesses, in insults, in hardships, in persecutions, in difficulties. For when I am weak, then I am strong."
2 Corinthians 12:9-10

———

"To do for yourself the best that you have it in you to do - to grit your teeth and clench your fists in order to survive the world at its harshest and worst - is, by that very act, to be unable to let something be done for you and in you that is more wonderful still. The trouble with steeling yourself against the harshness of reality is that the same steel that secures your life against being destroyed [further wounded] secures your life also against being opened up and transformed." - Frederick Beuechner, The Sacred Journey

———

5. **Discipleship reveals ways we may be thwarted by sin, wounds and warfare** (see Appendix C). Along the way in the sanctification process, a disciple may find themselves stuck, their progress impeded by sin, an emotional or spiritual wound or the attack of the enemy. Breakthrough in these areas is imperative for deeper growth. Healing prayer, spiritual direction and/or counseling overlay the entire discipleship process offering an avenue for greater intimacy with God and may be utilized many times as a disciple grows.

———

"If you feel frustrated because no matter how often you hear that God loves you, your heart - impervious to what you hear - believes God looks upon you with disappointment and anger ... I [we] want to help you identify the stones preventing God's love from reaching your heart and to help you seek God to tear them down - stone by stone - until your heart celebrates, knowing your Father not only loves you but delights in you." - Jasona Brown

———

As you look at these phases of spiritual growth, remember the growth process of a disciple is not formulaic and linear. These phases are not rigid categories; they are general ideas of the heart's movement on a relational path. We don't exist in any area completely; in some areas our faith is growing more than others. Much like our physical health, we have areas where we are healthy and others we need to improve. But we do have a primary "home," a phase where we are primarily living from and in. As we grow, we find ourselves dwelling more in the next phase than we did previously, and it becomes our new home. It is not unusual though for this movement to occasionally feel like it is going backward as we revisit previous struggles. But ultimately this takes us into deeper union with Jesus. The diagram on the following page seeks to illustrate this movement.

As you begin this journey, take the Discipleship Assessment at GreenwoodCC. com/discipleship, and then discuss your results with your leader/group.

Exploring
God is at work in our hearts, creating longing and curiosity about Jesus, and an openness to listen and learn about faith in Him. We are beginning to sense a need for the forgiveness of the Savior resulting in feelings of being excited and/ or conflicted.

Developing
Having been made alive in Jesus (regeneration), we have a new heart and a growing desire to know, trust and walk with Him. We are experiencing a thirst for God, the Bible and a community of faith.

Divided
At this phase, a disciple may hit a point where we are aware of the pull of the flesh and the world in opposition to the Spirit and the Kingdom. Our walk with God may be inconsistent, "up and down," and we may experience discouragement and doubt.

Deepening
This season is marked by our faith integrating into all areas of our life, and our hearts are marked by joy. Spiritual disciplines are part of our natural rhythms. We're able to stand firm in trials, with deep confidence and intimacy and we naturally tell others about Jesus and His Kingdom. We are joyfully and faithfully in the process of seeing and savoring Jesus in all moments of our daily life, becoming increasingly conformed to His image.

Flourishing

Longing to know and love God more moves us to seek more in our faith. We are seeking new ways of encountering Jesus through listening to the Spirit, meditating on the Word and deepening our prayer life. We are experiencing greater and greater joy and oneness with Jesus. We are actively investing in the lives of others, furthering the gospel and the Kingdom of God.

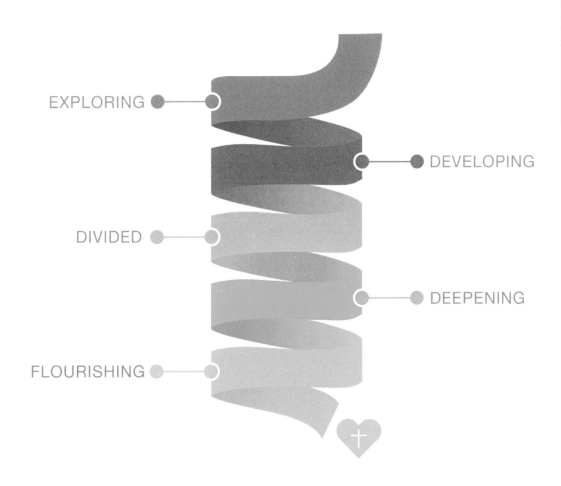

EXPLORING

DEVELOPING

DIVIDED

DEEPENING

FLOURISHING

──• LECTIO DIVINA

Luke 9:18-27

──• DISCUSSION QUESTIONS

1. After reflecting on the five foundational truths, which one do you most identify with, either now or in the past, and why?

2. Look at the diagonal of sanctification in Appendix B. The blue line indicates how God sees our growth. He views us through the completed work of Christ, as expressed in 2 Corinthians 5:17, "Therefore, if anyone is in Christ, he is a new creation; the old has gone, the new has come!" But we experience the reality of our growth as expressed in the green line. Is it difficult for you to reconcile these concepts? Has your experience of growth been consistent with the green line? How or how not? What remains the same in both lines?

3. Share your results from the Discipleship Assessment with one another. What surprised you? What encouraged you? In what area(s) do you see the opportunity for growth?

SESSION 3
The Starting Point: Good News!

. . . .

 "The Kingdom of heaven is like a treasure hidden in a field. When a man found it, he hid it again, and then in his joy went and sold all he had and bought that field." Matthew 13:44

"He [Jesus] comes where we are, and he brings us the life we hunger for. An early report reads, 'Life was in him, life that made sense of human existence' (John 1:4). To be the light of life, and to deliver God's life to women and men where they are and as they are, is the secret of the enduring relevance of Jesus. Suddenly they are flying right-side up, in a world that makes sense."
- Dallas Willard, The Divine Conspiracy

Jesus came announcing good news, and He described His offer as the very best treasure we could ever hope to find. If we could really see it, He said, we would be overcome with joy and do everything to arrange our lives to receive His offer.

If anything could really be this good, surely we don't want to miss it! Yet there is so much confusion, ignorance and even apathy about Jesus' good news that we would be wise to consider Jesus' offer at the beginning of our interaction with His invitations in this resource. Having a clear understanding of the good news (gospel) is crucial for living our lives as God intended when He created us. Our joy and commitment to following Jesus will be shaped by our vision of the kind of life God offers us in Jesus Christ.

When we read the Gospels, we see Jesus announcing a specific message of good news. Mark tells us, "After John was put in prison, Jesus went into Galilee proclaiming the good news of God. 'The time has come,' he said. 'The kingdom of God is near. Repent and believe the good news!'" (Mark 1:14-15, Matthew 4:23, Luke 4:43). Reading through the book of Acts confirms that the Apostles continued Jesus' announcement of the good news of the Kingdom of God (Acts 19:8, 20:25, 28:30-31).

The good news of the Kingdom of God is the announcement of a person and a fact. The person is Jesus. God has annointed Jesus as King (Messiah/Christ) and Eternal Son. The fact is that Jesus is bringing heaven - the Kingdom of God - to earth. Jesus has initiated God's great invasion of the earth, bringing His Life and gracious rule (the Kingdom of God). Taking all of Jesus' message together, we may think of the good news as follows:

The gospel of the Kingdom is the good news that in King Jesus, God is exercising His authority and power to rescue and restore repentant sinners to new life in His Kingdom now. He will eventually restore all things in a new heaven and earth under His rule.

"The need which the Christian faith answers is not so much that we are ignorant and need better information, but that we are lost and need someone to come and find us, stuck in the quicksand waiting to be rescued, dying and in need of new life." - Tom Wright, Simply Christian

So what does this have to do with salvation? In the New Testament "salvation" is a broad term meaning "rescue, deliverance, healing, wholeness and restoration." The terms "salvation," "eternal life" and "Kingdom of God" all refer to the same reality experienced by disciples of Jesus (Mark 10:17-27). The "salvation" that Jesus brings us is a new life with God in His Kingdom now and forever (John 10:10, Acts 5:20). "Eternal life" is the gift of a personally dynamic relationship with God where we experience His presence, love, rule and power in our lives starting now. We experience LIFE with Jesus (John 17:3, 1 John 5:11-12).

"For one to have the Kingdom of God is to have God, bound by an oath to save, employing all His love, power, and wisdom to give us freely all things and to pursue after us to do us good. But the greatest of all His gifts is that fellowship with him." - Daniel Fuller, The Unity of the Bible

When it is said of Jesus, "He will save his people from their sins" (Matthew 1:21), it means that He saves us from more than the consequences of our sin. Salvation is much more than a change in our legal status before God. Salvation through Jesus always means being saved *from* sin and *for* God. Through Jesus, God gives us forgiveness of our sins and rescues us from the penalty of our sin, which is separation from God (Acts 10:36, Ephesians 1:7). He rescues us from the power of sin to dominate our lives (John 8:31-36, Romans 8:9-11). He rescues us from Satan's cruel and deceptive rule over us (Acts 26:17-18, Colossians 1:13-14).

But we are also saved for relationship with Him. He restores us into a loving relationship with God as our King and Father (Luke 12:32-34, 2 Corinthians 5:17-21). He gives us the Holy Spirit as God's empowering presence in us and with us as well as a guarantee of life forever in God's Kingdom (Acts 2:38-39, 1 Corinthians 1:8-9, Ephesians 1:13-15). He promises us resurrection bodies fit for the new heaven and earth when King Jesus returns to make all things new (Matthew 19:28-30, 1 Corinthians 15, Revelation 21:5). And He calls us to be His friends and allies in bringing the Kingdom to earth. All of this is salvation or eternal life, which is life with God now and in His Kingdom forever.

"Jesus' good news - his gospel - is simply this: the Kingdom of God has now, through Jesus, become available for ordinary human beings to live in. It's here. Now. You can live in it if you want to. ... God is present here and now. God is acting. You can revise your plans for living around this cosmic opportunity to daily experience God's favor and power." - John Ortberg, Eternity is Now in Session

------

You may wonder what is the relationship between the good news of the Kingdom and the death and resurrection of Jesus? The reason the gospel is so often summarized in the death and resurrection of King Jesus is that these were the defining events of His life that make the Kingdom of God available to us now and forever (1 Corinthians 15:1-8). The death of King Jesus is the way God satisfies His justice so He can forgive our sins (Romans 3:21-26). The resurrection of Jesus is the way God demonstrates Jesus to be His Eternal Son and King as well as the way we gain access into life with God (Romans 1:1-6). The right response required of us to receive the gift of life with God in His Kingdom is repentance and faith (Mark 1:14-15, Luke 24:45-49, Acts 2:38-39).

Repentance is our turning to live our lives centered in Jesus and the Kingdom of God rather than in ourselves and our kingdom. Faith is entrusting ourselves to King Jesus as God's Son and Savior for new life in His Kingdom now and forever. Our faith is not merely in believing or doing the right things, but in the person of Jesus (1 John 5:12).

Hopefully, starting this guide with a clear view of Jesus' good news helps us see how the gospel is so much more than the call to believe the right things so God will let us into heaven when we die. Jesus' good news is more than trusting an arrangement He has secured. Unfortunately, this popular view of Christianity has left too many deceived and falling short of the beautiful gift offered by God through Jesus. Jesus has never called us simply to believe the right things so we can live as "consumers of His merit with God." Instead He has called us to come to Him and trust Him. As we trust Him, we will commit ourselves to follow and obey Him as His disciples.

Jesus models and teaches us a way of living attentively to God's Presence and priorities. His invitations and commands are the way we experience this new life with God in His Kingdom and how we live as His friends and allies in bringing the Kingdom (John 7:16-17, 8:31-32, 15:1-17). As we prepare to engage with these invitations of Jesus, let us consider the importance of taking them seriously as the "obedience that comes from faith" (Romans 1:5).

———

"To 'trust Jesus' in the Gospels simply means to think he is right - about everything - and therefore to be ready to do what he says, not as a means of getting into the good place but as the best advice from the wisest person possible. In fact, it's only as we seek to do what Jesus says - to be generous and forgiving and radically truthful - that we discover the Kingdom he talks about is real and can be trusted.

...

"The reason Jesus calls us to obey him is not so that we can earn our way into heaven. ... Obedience - rightly understood - is what a saved life looks like from the inside. Saving faith is faith that allows me to engage in interactive, grace-powered life with him beginning here and now, which death will then be powerless to interrupt. It's faith that allows me to know union with Christ."
- John Ortberg, Eternity is Now in Session

———

"My teaching is not my own. It comes from him who sent me. If anyone chooses to do God's will, he will find out whether my teaching comes from God or whether I speak on my own. ... If you hold to my teaching, you are really my disciples. Then you will know the truth, and the truth will set you free."
- Jesus, John 7:16-17, 8:31-32

"Come to me, all you who are weary and burdened, and I will give you rest. Take my yoke upon you and learn from me, for I am gentle and humble in heart, and you will find rest for your souls. For my yoke is easy and my burden is light."
- Jesus, Matthew 11:28-30

—• LECTIO DIVINA

Matthew 4:12-25

—• DISCUSSION QUESTIONS

1. How does this introduction to the gospel differ from what you have heard or believed? What about the concepts of "salvation" and "eternal life"?

2. What thoughts, feelings or questions does this introduction to the gospel stir in you?

3. Revelation 3:20 says, "Here I am! I stand at the door and knock. If anyone hears my voice and opens the door, I will come in and eat with him, and he with me." God is knocking, calling all of us to come and follow Him. Have you ever responded to God's invitation and given your life to Jesus? This is not just believing the "right" things about God. It is receiving the invitation to follow Jesus and His ways. If you have not taken this step but feel called to now, simply say something like this in your own words: "God, I need you! I confess my sin and pride to you. Forgive me of all my sins and for trying to do it by myself. I declare that Jesus is my Lord and Savior. And now help me to live with You and for You as Your disciple. I pray this in Jesus' name. Amen." If you prayed this, share your experience with your group.

4. If you have already given your life to Jesus, share when and how that new life began.

THE INVITATIONS OF JESUS
Introduction

. . . .

You are invited, welcomed, desired and called to enter into a journey of loving and following King Jesus. This life-long journey has a rhythm of worship and prayer, community and mission with nine foundational invitations. This is the joy-filled life of a disciple of Jesus.

⟶• WORSHIP AND PRAYER

In worship and prayer, we cultivate an attentive life to God's Presence in Jesus. Attention is the beginning of adoration. Through worship and prayer, the Holy Spirit helps us to see God's beauty, love and goodness. We have our hearts opened to His love and grace so we can love Him and others with His love. Worship and prayer are the fuel for experiencing LIFE with Jesus.

Worship and prayer are the fuel for experiencing LIFE with Jesus.

Come
Jesus invites us to come to Him, welcoming us as we are, to experience all of who He is and the radical transformation of life in Him.

Know
Jesus invites us to know God intimately and who He says we are as His sons/ daughters. This knowing is vital and life-giving to live into the role He has for us in the Kingdom.

Breathe
Jesus invites us to live empowered by the Holy Spirit and abiding in Him.

⟶• COMMUNITY

Jesus calls us out of the individualism and isolation of our age so that we may experience God's love through one another. He calls us to share our lives together to reflect the LIFE that has existed eternally in God as Father, Son and Holy Spirit. In community we share life together to encourage each other towards faithfulness to Jesus. Community is the context for experiencing LIFE with Jesus.

Together

Jesus invites us to Himself, calling us into the community of His disciples. This life together is the context of discipleship and the way we practically obey His command to love one another.

Conversation

Jesus invites us into a life built on prayer - intimate, corporate, listening, confessing and healing conversations with the Father guided by the Spirit.

Rest

Jesus invites us to live a counter-cultural daily rest of abiding in Him for all our needs and a Sabbath rest to fuel our lives.

> Community is the context for experiencing LIFE with Jesus.

⟶ MISSION

Jesus came to rescue and restore broken hearts, lives and communities, and He sends His people on the same mission. Living on mission we serve and love our lost and broken world to bring God's LIFE for us through the life, death and resurrection of Jesus. Mission is the natural overflow of experiencing LIFE with Jesus.

> Mission is the natural overflow of experiencing LIFE with Jesus.

Serve

Jesus invites us to serve because He first served us through His radical love so that we can serve others within the church and then to the least of these.

Give

Jesus invites and frees us to live joyfully generous lives for His Kingdom.

Go

Jesus invites us to "go" on mission with Him, empowered by the Holy Spirit, rescuing and restoring our lost and broken world back to God.

THE INVITATIONS OF JESUS

WORSHIP & PRAYER

- COME
- KNOW
- BREATHE

· ·

Jesus invites us to come to Him, welcoming us as we are to experience all of Who He is and the radical transformation of life in Him.

STORY
a personal story with fictional names

Jesus' invitation to us comes in many different ways. Jennifer is the oldest of four daughters, raised by a single mom. She was not raised in a home that embraced faith in God. From an early age she learned that in order to survive and have an easier life than her mom had, she needed to work hard and take control of her life. It wasn't until many years later, when her son was three years old, that she felt God lightly knocking on the door of her heart. They were on a family vacation and as they walked along the beach, gazing at stunning sunsets and breathing in the refreshing sea breeze, several questions kept bubbling up such as, "Is this all there is to life?"; "Why am I here?"; "What is my purpose in life?".

After the vacation was over they returned to the hustle and bustle of daily life, those questions faded away ... until several years later. Jennifer was invited to church by a friend from work who was steadfast in his love and faith in God and guided her towards the love of God. For the first time she heard more about Jesus and His love for her. The old stirrings in her heart were resurrected as she would go to church each week to worship and hear sermons. As she heard more of God's love for her, tears would flow freely. She soon realized the emptiness of trying to take control of her life and decided to give her life to Jesus. When she was baptized, she said, "I repent from my sins and I have surrendered control of my life to Jesus Christ, so that I may live with the love and grace in God's kingdom everlasting." God, first called Jennifer by putting "eternity into her heart" through deep life questions and then slowly inviting her to COME to Him, the author and completer of life.

STUDY

Most people are living the dance between intimacy with God or hiding from God. We either know that we are created and loved by God or we hide in our self-reliance or shame. In fact, Adam and Eve first experienced the sweet intimacy of being created, known and loved in the first two chapters of the Bible. By the third chapter of Genesis, they were hiding. Thankfully, God did not leave them in their shame; He pursued them by saying, "Where are you?" (Genesis 3:9).

We were created to be with God and yet we, like Adam and Eve, often hide. Throughout the pages of the Old Testament, it illustrates the dance of the Israelites following Him or following the gods of the surrounding nations. And yet, throughout that dance, God pursues them with the hope that "I will take you as my own people, and I will be your God" (Exodus 6:7).

The greatest reflection of God's pursuit for us is the life, death and resurrection of Jesus Christ. God became man and said, "Come, follow me" (Matthew 4:19). This is the echo of God calling out in the garden, "Where are you?" He is inviting us just as we are. His invitation is not dependent on how good we are or even how messed up we are. It is totally dependent on His love for us.

And that love does not leave us to ourselves. It is an invitation to experience all of who He is - His love, joy, peace, patience, kindness, goodness, faithfulness, gentleness and self-control (Galatians 5:22-23). His invitation to encounter Him is extended so that we might experience the radical transformation of life in Him.

To learn more about how to read and study God's word, see Appendix D.

READ
Deuteronomy 30:19-20, John 10:1-10

HEAD
Deuteronomy 30 is Moses' last words to the Israelites before they cross over into the promised land. God rescued them from Egypt, they wandered in the wilderness for 40 years and now they are finally entering the promised land. How did the Israelites hear these words in this passage? When God says, "Now choose life," how do you think God defines "life"?

In John 10, Jesus uses the imagery of a shepherd and a flock to depict His care and love for His sheep, the people of God. What do we learn about Jesus from the illustration of Him as the Good Shepherd?

HEART

In Deuteronomy 30, when you read, "Now choose life," do you hear God's love, His anger or His compassion? If you were to die today and be in God's presence, would God be disappointed in you, angry at you or welcome you with love? Why?

In John 10, Jesus' sheep are those who enter through Him and know His voice. "The sheep listen to His voice" (v. 3) and "His sheep follow Him because they know His voice" (v. 4). Do you feel like you "know His voice"? What does it mean to "know His voice"?

HANDS

God's invitation of "come, follow me" is a daily invitation. It is foundational to establish life-giving daily rhythms in the Word, prayer and worship. With those in your group, share what you are currently doing for daily spiritual rhythms. Is there an area you could grow in? If you are a parent, how are you teaching and modeling these spiritual rhythms to your kids?

SPIRITUAL EXERCISE

This week start each day by saying the Lord's Prayer.
See Appendix E for a contemplative Lord's Prayer.

LECTIO DIVINA

John 10:1-10

MEMORY VERSE

John 10:10

"The thief comes only to steal and kill and destroy; I have come that
they may have life, and have it to the full."

. . . .

Jesus invites us to know God intimately and who He says we are as His sons/daughters. This knowing is vital and life-giving to live into the role He has for us in the Kingdom.

STORY
a personal story with fictional names

Even as a little girl, Kate remembers clinging to words of affirmation and being crushed by failure and criticism. Kate was a dancer and her life revolved around performance and mirrors. As she became an adult, Kate's identity was formed - really it was malformed - around appearance and applause. And it was never enough to fill her heart. For the next decade, she struggled with a secret eating disorder and sank deeper into hiding and insecurity.

Kate gave her life to Jesus in her teen years and thought that if she obeyed Him perfectly, she would gain a sense of who she was and truly feel loved. That didn't work and she sank deeper into despair. It wasn't until she was a young mother battling her addiction, fear and failure that she began to address the issue of true identity.

A wise woman came alongside Kate to disciple her and helped Kate see that underneath her addiction, fear and perfectionism was a false narrative about who she was. As this woman prayed with Kate and read words of truth from Scripture about identity in Christ, Kate's heart was flooded with His love and slowly she began to believe that Jesus spoke words of truth about her identity. The words of others and the experiences of her life that formerly had told her she wasn't valued or even ok were disarmed and His words took their place. As she matured and grew, and as the Spirit strengthened her identity, Kate became who God had created her to be and walked into freedom from addiction and perfectionism. She no longer obeyed and performed for identity, but rather received it from Jesus. And in that freedom Kate stepped into the role He had designed for her in His Kingdom.

STUDY

"Your real, new self (which is Christ's and also yours, and yours just because it is His) will not come as long as you are looking for it. It will come when you are looking for Him." - *C.S. Lewis, Mere Christianity*

One of the most common and perplexing questions in life is, "Who am I?" We look all around us for the answer to that question, taking identity from people and defining ourselves through experiences. The true answer to the question of our identity lies in the heart of God. As we know Jesus for who He really is, the One who loves us and created us, then we will know ourselves for who we really are and we will live obediently out of the security of being known and loved by our Father. Augustine prays, "Lord, let me know myself; let me know you." This "double knowledge" - knowing the Lord and knowing ourselves - is the basis for our growth in maturity and faith.

Covenant (relationship) and Kingdom (responsibility) are kinds of spiritual DNA, seen throughout the Bible. In the beginning we had relational wholeness with God which was broken by rebellion, resulting in our alienation from Him. But through His grace and mercy, God initiated relationship restoration and healing through Jesus. He invites us into this covenant relationship with His Father, where we experience being fully known and loved.

The Covenant triangle shape gives us a way to "see" this covenantal relationship in our lives. It begins with the Father telling us our identity and then obedience follows which gives glory to the Father. But often we work "backward" by trying to obey in order to gain identity or worth (being a good Christian) and then believing this obedience earns His love.

FATHER

COVENANT

OBEDIENCE   IDENTITY

God gives us our true identity as His children, a beloved son or daughter. As our Creator, He is the one who can tell His creation who they are. Out of that identity flows obedience. Our obedience does not give us identity; it reveals our identity.

We choose to obey Him because this is the most consistent way of expressing our identity as beloved children of God. The Holy Spirit fills us and gives us grace for both the ability and the freedom to obey God, uniting our hearts with His to experience all His love, goodness and joy.

The Kingdom triangle expresses how our new life is lived under His authority as friends and allies of King Jesus. As followers of Jesus we are now citizens of heaven, partakers in His Kingdom. We worship and seek to revere Jesus as King over all areas of our lives. We acknowledge God is the majestic Ruler of heaven and earth, and He seeks to extend His loving rule through the lives of all people.

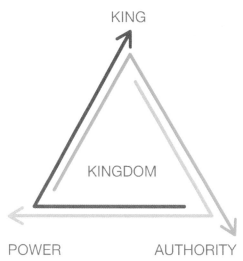

As King, God clearly has the authority to act, but remarkably He expresses His authority through His people, giving them the responsibility of representing Him. As the Creator and Sustainer of the universe, God has incredible and all-encompassing power. He chooses to use this power to express His love to people and, more surprisingly, through people who carry His authority as King. We must live in obedience to Him as King and in surrendered faith in order to move out in His power, obeying His Great Commission and Command to love, serve, share the Gospel and to participate in His restoration of all things.

Again, we can make the mistake of moving "backward," using power without living under the King's authority.

Covenant and Kingdom Triangles developed by 3DM.

READ
Matthew 3:16-17, Matthew 16:13-20, Matthew 28:16-20

HEAD

In Matthew 3:17, what words of identity did God speak over Jesus? Why do you think God did this? What do you think the people who heard this felt?

How did Peter answer the question of Jesus' identity in Matthew 16:16? Then who did Jesus say Peter was? How do you see this conversation in relation to the covenant triangle?

Looking at Matthew 28:16-20, what authority does Jesus give to His disciples? How does He ask us to move out in power? What has been your experience in this area ? What holds you back?

HEART

Think back over your life. Remember the words of others from events, accomplishments or failures. Did these create true identity in line with God's Word or false identity? Where have you found identity?

How has this shaped you, what you believe and how you live?

Read the identity verses in Appendix F. Which verse speaks to your heart?

HANDS
Read the attributes of God in Appendix G. What attribute is He highlighting for you?

Pray and ask the Spirit to imprint the truth of who He is and of your identity on your heart and to reveal His plan for you in His Kingdom.

SPIRITUAL EXERCISE
Listen to Lauren Daigle's song *You Say*. Journal your response as a prayer of gratitude as the beloved son/daughter of God.

LECTIO DIVINA
1 Peter 2:9-10

MEMORY VERSE
Isaiah 43:1

"But now, this is what the Lord says —
he who created you, Jacob,
he who formed you, Israel:
'Do not fear, for I have redeemed you;
I have summoned you by name; you are mine.'"

· ·

Jesus invites us to live empowered by the Holy Spirit and abiding in Him.

STORY
a true story as told by Daniel Henderson

———

"Regardless of your theological journey in connection to the Holy Spirit, you might need to overcome one major factor in your past. I'll be the first to confess this one. We have a tendency to live independently of the Holy Spirit. We just don't sense a deep and consistent need for Him. My friend, Robbie Symons, summarized it well: 'We need to stop trying and start relying!'

Charles Spurgeon, perhaps the greatest and most widely-read preacher of recent centuries, exemplified a humble reliance on the Holy Spirit. His ministry, based at the Metropolitan Tabernacle in London in the late 1800s, resulted in scores of thousands of people coming to Christ along with the launching of an orphanage and a pastor's college. As he mounted the pulpit each week to preach to thousands, he silently declared to his own heart, with each of the fifteen steps, "I believe in the Holy Spirit. I believe in the Holy Spirit. I believe in the Holy Spirit." Spurgeon wrote: 'Without the Spirit of God we can do nothing; we are as ships without wind or chariots without steeds; like branches without sap, we are withered; like coals without fire, we are useless; as an offering without a sacrificial flame, we are unaccepted.'"

———

STUDY

———

"You might as well try to see without eyes, hear without ears, or breathe without lungs, as try to live the Christian life without the Holy Spirit." - D.L. Moody

———

Yet many of us try to live the Christian life without the Holy Spirit. Instead of living daily relying on the power of the Holy Spirit, we turn to our own strength. Here's the great news: living a life of faith isn't left up to you. You have the Holy Spirit within you to empower you to live! But there's a lot of confusion about who the Holy Spirit is even among Christians. According to a recent study of evangelical Christians conducted by Lifeway Research, when asked about the Holy Spirit:

· 56% said the Holy Spirit is a force rather than a person
· 28% said the Spirit is a divine being, but not equal to God the Father and Jesus
· 21% said they were not sure

Confusion about the Holy Spirit and our relationship with Him is not just an intellectual, theological problem. Without a clear understanding of the Spirit - who He is and how we relate to Him - we will have a diminished experience of the love and joy of Jesus and the power to flourish based on His work and promises, especially when facing life's challenges.

Who is the Holy Spirit?

The Holy Spirit is fully God, sent by the Father to regenerate, indwell, empower, grow and gift every believer for the glory of Jesus.

In John 14:16, Jesus begins to teach about our relationship with the Holy Spirit. And in John 16:5-7, He tells the disciples that it will be good for them when He leaves because the Spirit will come. Jesus is saying that the Spirit in them is better than Jesus with them. The same is true for us.

When He was alive on Earth, Jesus was limited to time and space. The Spirit is NOT. The Spirit brings the abiding Presence of God within us. We think we are limited by our weakness or ability. The Spirit is NOT. Our weakness is not an obstacle for the Spirit, rather it is an opportunity. God wants you to know the power to heal, the power to press on, the power to love and minister, the power to obey - *any* power you need - does not come from within you, but from within the *Spirit in you*. And if God's power is in you, then you have an infinite, merciful and invincible strength that will keep you and grow you in every circumstance. His divine power is for you, not against you. The Holy Spirit indwells you, bringing your heart into deeper oneness with Jesus and empowering you to live with Him and look more and more like Him.

What does it look like to walk in the Spirit? It is moment by moment surrender, a spiritual breathing, filling us. We surrender (like exhaling) and admit our total dependence on Him, our weakness and need, confessing any sin or struggle. Then we seek Him, inviting Him to fill us (like inhaling) and we intentionally focus, redirecting our hearts and minds through His Word, worship and prayer. This is the life of abiding in the power of the Holy Spirit which manifests His holiness in our lives.

Although we may experience a tremendous breakthrough in areas of struggle, we will still experience struggle. Just as we still literally stumble and trip while walking, as imperfect people we will "stumble" as we walk in the Spirit. And gratefully God knows and understands this, and He is faithful.

READ
John 15:5, 16:6-7, 13-15; Romans 8:5-17, Galatians 5:22-23

HEAD
Make a list of all you discover about the Spirit in the verses in John, Romans and Galatians. It will be extensive! What excites you? Note anything that puzzles you.

HEART

What has your understanding of the Spirit been thus far in your journey? Do you desire more intimacy with Jesus? Ask the Spirit to fill you with His love.

HANDS

Is there an area of your life where you are experiencing significant struggle? Write a prayer confessing and asking the Spirit for the grace you need to walk in obedience. Share this with your discipleship group (James 5:16.) Close with these words from Romans 15:13: "May the God of hope fill you with all joy and peace as you trust in Him, so that you may overflow with hope by the power of the Holy Spirit."

SPIRITUAL EXERCISE

Quiet yourself before the Lord. Listen to His heart of love for you. Acknowledge the Presence of God within you, His Spirit. If you desire to deepen your relationship with the Holy Spirit, here is a suggested prayer by *Francis Chan* in *The Forgotten God*:

"Spirit, we know that we have done wrong by You. Please forgive us for grieving, resisting, and quenching You. We have resisted You through sin, through our rebellion, and through our hardness of heart. At times, we have been spiritually blind. At other times, we knew what You wanted us to do, but we chose to ignore Your promptings. Yet this is not how we want to live now. We need You to change us.

Only through You can we truly worship. Spirit of the Lord, You are the one who brings us to a place where we can worship. You are the Spirit of truth, the Spirit of holiness, the Spirit of life. Thank You for the truth, the holiness, and the life You give us.

We need Your wisdom and understanding as we seek to live this life. Keep us from disbelief, from fear. We need Your strength to help us do what You are asking us to do and to live how You are asking us to live. Speak loudly and drown out the other voices calling us to conform to the patterns of this world.

You are the Spirit of self-control and love. Give us the self-control needed to deny our flesh and follow You. Give us a love strong enough to motivate courageous action. Manifest Yourself through us that we may serve and love Your bride, the church, as You do.

Come, Holy Spirit, come. We don't know exactly what that means and looks like for each of us yet, in the particular places You've called us to inhabit. But, nonetheless, whatever it means, we ask for Your presence. Come, Holy Spirit, come. Amen."

LECTIO DIVINA
John 14:15-31

MEMORY VERSE
Romans 5:5

"And hope does not put us to shame, because God's love has been poured out into our hearts through the Holy Spirit, who has been given to us."

THE INVITATIONS OF JESUS

COMMUNITY

- TOGETHER
- CONVERSATION
- REST

TOGETHER
Community . The Invitations of Jesus

. . . .

Jesus invites us to Himself, calling us into the community of His disciples. This life together is the context of discipleship and the way we practically obey His command to love one another.

STORY
a true story as told in a popular movie

The movie *Antwone Fisher* is the true story of a U.S. sailor's journey of overcoming self-destructive hatred by the faithful love of a father figure in the person of a Navy psychologist. The opening scene of the movie is a recurring dream Antwone has of being a young boy welcomed by his ancestors into a loving family where he belongs. The dream abruptly ends, and we discover that Antwone is a troubled young sailor in danger of being discharged for his violent behavior. As the story progresses, we learn the backstory of abuse and abandonment that is the root of his rage and poor self-image.

Fortunately, Antwone is not left to battle his wounds alone. A Navy psychologist keeps loving Antwone, offering to share his life with him and speaking wisdom and grace into his heart. Because of the love of this father figure, Antwone gains the courage to work through his rage and abandonment. He even develops the courage to find some of his family. At the end of the movie, Antwone is welcomed into a family he never knew existed. He is a man who is maturing because he has been loved well.

The movie is a beautiful picture of the way God's love aims to bring us home to Himself and into His family. Like Antwone, we all experience some struggles to love and be loved. God's primary design is to call us into His family, pour His love into our hearts and then call us to love one another with the love He gives us.

STUDY
────

"The life of faith revealed and nurtured in biblical narratives is highly personal but never merely individual. ... God's love and salvation are revealed and experienced in the congregation of the people. ... The gospel pulls us into community. One of the immediate changes the

gospel makes is grammatical: we instead of I; our instead of my; us instead of me. ... The same salvation that restores our relationship with God reinstates us in the community of persons who live by faith. ... A believing community is the context for the life of faith. ... The life of faith always and necessarily takes place in a community of persons who are located somewhere in time and place."
- Eugene Peterson, Reversed Thunder

———

Many of us, if we're honest, find Jesus' call into community surprising and maybe inconvenient. If we have grown up in the Western hemisphere, we have been immersed and formed by a culture of radical individualism. We naturally view our relationship with Jesus through this lens, which leaves us with a very privatized view of the life of faith. Add in the busyness of our lives and the quirky nature of people, and many of us might just prefer a life with Jesus alone.

In the quote above, Eugene Peterson challenges our typical way of thinking about the gospel and faith. He reminds us that in the Bible, believing and belonging always go together. Paul expressed this spiritual principle saying, "So in Christ we who are many form one Body, and each member belongs to all the others" (Romans 12:5). The Bible presents a clear and consistent message. The Lord's call to us is always personal, but never private. He calls us as individual persons, but He always calls us to be "the people of God" - a community of persons living by faith with Him at the center.

Why is God's design and call to do life together?

1. Life together expresses the heart of God because it is the nature of God. God has ultimately been revealed to us as One God in a community of three Persons: Father, Son and Holy Spirit. These three Persons have existed eternally in a perfect community of love, joy, creativity and purpose (John 17:1-5, 2 Corinthians 13:14). The Triune God is fundamentally a relational Being, so John writes "God is love" and "let us love one another because love comes from God" (1 John 4:7, 16). Everything in the Christian life is intended to reflect God's glory including His relational nature.

2. Life together is the only practical way we can obey Jesus' command that we "love one another" as He has loved us (John 13:34-35). If we have experienced God's love through Jesus Christ, we will desire to obey Jesus by loving our Christian brothers and sisters with God's love (1 John 4:7-12). One of the most basic, tangible expressions of our faith is loving one another (Galatians 5:6). There is no practical way to love another apart from meaningful relationship with one another. Consider the practical ways we are commanded to love one another:

"be devoted to one another" (Romans 12:10); "rejoice and weep with one another" (Romans 12:15); "instruct one another" (Romans 15:14); "be kind and compassionate to one another, forgiving each other just as Christ forgave you" (Ephesians 4:32); "teach and admonish one another" (Colossians 3:16); "serve one another" (Galatians 5:13); "carry one another's burdens" (Galatians 6:2); "comfort one another" (2 Corinthians 1:4); "encourage one another" (1 Thessalonians 5:11); "submit to one another" (Ephesians 5:21); "confess your sins to one another and pray for one another" (James 5:16); "encourage one another daily ... so that none of you may be hardened by sin's deceitfulness" (Hebrews 3:13); "spur one another on towards love and good deeds. Let us not give up meeting together as some are in the habit of doing ..." (Hebrews 10:24-25).

3. Life together is the best context for spiritual growth as we experience God's love, truth and grace in safe, authentic, loving and praying relationships with Jesus at the center (Ephesians 4:1-16). As we "open our hearts to one another" (2 Corinthians 6:11-13), we are better able to experience God's transforming love and grace and appropriate His truth in our lives. Obviously, this does not happen very well in a crowd of isolated individuals, but rather in a community of people committed to sharing life together with Jesus at the center.

READ
John 13:34-35, 1 John 4:7-12

In John's letter (1 John), the Apostle is writing to followers of Jesus who are in danger of being deceived by false teaching (1 John 4:1) as well as seduced by the sinful enticements of their surrounding culture (1 John 2:15-17). His purpose in writing is to call them to faithful discipleship to Jesus and offer them the way they can be assured they belong to Jesus (1 John 5:13). One of the ways they can know they have been born again of the Holy Spirit is their intention to love their Christian brothers and sisters (1 John 1:3-6, 3:14-15, 4:7, 5:1).

HEAD

Twice in this passage, John instructs us that we should love one another, meaning our Christian brothers and sisters (1 John 4:7, 11). What are the reasons he gives for our motivation to love one another?

John also connects our commitment to love one another to certain spiritual truths about us (1 John 4:7-8). What does he say our willingness or lack of willingness to love indicates?

Jesus and John identify very specific ways that Jesus and God the Father showed their love to us (John 13:34, 1 John 4:9-10). What specific actions by Jesus and God the Father are identified? What does this indicate about the kind of love we are called to? How does this differ from the way our culture thinks of love?

HEART

Consider 1 John 4:9-10 and Romans 5:5-8. Can you remember the first time you realized that God loved you so much that He sent His Son Jesus as an atoning sacrifice for your sin?

Read Ephesians 3:14-19. Can you remember a specific time when you were experientially aware of God's love for you? On a scale of 1-10, how much do you live with a deep sense that you are loved by God in Jesus Christ? How does this motivate and empower you to love others?

HANDS

Evaluate your present commitment to share life intimately with some fellow disciples of Jesus. Are you a part of a small group of disciples that seek to love one another? What has been your experience of this life together? If you are not, are you willing to obey Jesus in this manner?

How might your present Christian relationships move toward a more faithful embodiment of the various "one another" commands in the New Testament (see Scriptures above)?

A SPIRITUAL EXERCISE

Watch the movie *Antwone Fisher* and ask the Holy Spirit to help you see any ways this story reflects anything about your own story. What has been your experience with relationships in your family of origin, in school, marriage, etc.? Can you see any patterns that could possibly cause you to be reluctant to give yourself to others relationally?

Make Paul's prayer in Ephesians 3:14-19 your daily prayer for a while. Ask the Holy Spirit to show you any barriers to your ability to experience God's love more deeply.

LECTIO DIVINA
Mark 2:1-12

MEMORY VERSE
John 13:34-35

"A new command I give you: Love one another. As I have loved you, so you must love one another. By this all men will know that you are my disciples, if you love one another."

CONVERSATION
Community . The Invitations of Jesus

. . . .

Jesus invites us into a life built on prayer: intimate, corporate, listening, confessing and healing conversations with the Father, guided by the Spirit.

STORY
a personal story with fictional names

Prayer starts simply as a conversation with God. Lewis was a young boy who walked to school with his dad and little brother every day. They would find rocks to throw and sticks to use as swords along the way. The last section of their walk was through an apartment complex and finally to the gate across from the school where their father would see them off. Every time, he left them with the words, "Talk to Jesus throughout the day." Every single time, "Talk to Jesus throughout the day." For Lewis and his brother, it was just a thing their dad said and they didn't think much of it. But like a slow, steady river carving through a canyon, these words carved an image in these boys' minds and souls of a God they could talk to and who actually cares.

At first for these boys, their prayers would be about help with an upcoming test or a quick prayer as they came up to bat in a baseball game. And it soon grew to asking for help with anxiety and depression, to praying to God with others as a family and in church and even stopping to listen and enjoy His presence. Now Lewis often finds himself talking to Jesus on his back deck while looking at the morning light flickering off the leaves as the birds fill the air with a sweet song. He is married and has two little boys and as they get on the bus to school, he says to them every single time, "Talk to Jesus throughout the day."

STUDY

Jesus invites us into conversation with Him. In comparison to other world religions, where God is distant and all effort is made to reach him, the God of the Bible initiates and speaks to us and we can speak to Him. God first spoke the words "let there be light," and there was light (Genesis 1:3). God spoke to Adam and Eve, Cain and Abel, Enoch, Noah, Abraham, a maidservant named Hagar, Isaac, Jacob, the prophets and many others. Then, God's word became flesh in the form of Jesus (John 1). Jesus connects us with God, intercedes on our behalf (Romans 8:34) and is our great high priest. "Let us then approach the throne of grace with confidence, so that we may receive mercy and find grace to help us in our time of need" (Hebrews 4:16). Our conversations with God come in various forms of prayer: intimate, corporate, listening, confessing and healing prayer, all guided by the Holy Spirit.

- Intimate prayer is individually praying to God wherever and whenever (Matthew 6:6).
- Corporate prayer is the family of God praying together. From the early church, we see the absolute necessity of prayer when the church gathers (Acts 1:14, 24, 2:42, 3:1, 4:24).
- Listening prayer is the process of quieting one's heart and allowing God to speak, "But when he, the Spirit of truth, comes, he will guide you into all truth. He will not speak on his own; he will speak only what he hears …" (John 16:13).
- Confessing prayer is true repentance in response to our sin and brokenness in contrast to God's pure holiness and transformative grace (2 Corinthians 7:10, 1 John 1:9).
- Healing prayer speaks words of life and healing into the brokenness of our lives (sins, wounds, warfare and frailty). See Appendix C and I.

This privilege of conversation with God should not be taken for granted. In fact, if Jesus prioritized prayer with God, how much more should we? As Mark 1:35 says, "Very early in the morning, while it was still dark, Jesus got up, left the house and went off to a solitary place, where he prayed."

The Lord seems to have invested a greater measure of power in our prayers when we pray in unity together (Matthew 18:19-20). He has commanded that together we be a "house of prayer" (Matthew 21:12-13). The witness of the church in the Book of Acts, as well as throughout church history, is that the Lord is pleased to hear His people crying out together in faith and unity (Acts 2, 4, 12). The agony and the ecstasy of following Jesus, as we long for His Kingdom to be fully realized on earth, is designed by Him to be lived in the beautiful mess of a praying community.

READ
1 Samuel 1:1-2:2, Matthew 6:5-13

HEAD

In 1 Samuel 1, there is a powerful and intimate story of Hannah who is barren, crying out to God for a son. Why was barrenness such a burden to Hannah? What did Hannah's intimacy with God look like?

In Matthew 6, Jesus teaches on prayer. Whose prayers did Jesus denounce and why? What is different in the way that Jesus commands us to pray? What does it mean to call God "Our Father"?

Looking at the list of the different types of prayer, which is a strength for you? Which type is an area for growth?

HEART

For Hannah, the burden of barrenness weighed upon her soul. She explained to Eli, "I was pouring out my soul to the Lord" (1 Samuel 1:15). Have you ever had a burden that weighed on your soul? Did you cry out to God? What was His response?

When Jesus taught His disciples to pray, He told them to refer to God as "Our Father." Do you see God as your good, heavenly father? A distant task-master? Or something else? Why do you think you see God that way?

HANDS

Just as Jesus prioritized prayer in His life, we need to as well. If you don't already do so, start each day with prayer. Possibly read or memorize a prayer like the Lord's Prayer (Matthew 6:9-13) or a Psalm (18:1-3, 34, 96:1-6, 100, 103).

If you are a parent, what does prayer look like in your family? Do you pray before a meal? Do you pray before the kids head off to school? Is there something new you can do to be modeling prayer to your kids?

Sometimes it can be difficult to sit and pray; the mind easily wanders. If that is the case, try prayer walking. Find a nice path (i.e., Highline Canal) or a park and walk while you pray.

SPIRITUAL EXERCISE

Take an hour this week to go through the Immauel Moment listening prayer exercise (see Appendix H).

For more information about healing prayer, refer to Appendix I.

LECTIO DIVINA

Matthew 6:5-15

MEMORY VERSE

Philippians 4:6-7

"Do not be anxious about anything, but in every situation, by prayer and petition, with thanksgiving, present your requests to God. And the peace of God, which transcends all understanding, will guard your hearts and your minds in Christ Jesus."

REST
Community . The Invitations of Jesus

. . . .

Jesus invites us to live a counter-cultural daily rest of abiding in Him for all our needs and a Sabbath rest to fuel our lives.

STORY
a story from Howard Butt Jr. of Laity Lodge Retreat Center as written on TheologyofWork.org

―――――

"From 1916 to 1939, Justice Louis Brandeis sat on the U.S. Supreme Court. Once, right before the start of an important trial, Justice Brandeis took a short vacation - and drew heavy criticism for it. But Brandeis delivered an excellent defense. "I need rest," he said. "I find that I can do a year's work in eleven months, but I can't do it in twelve."

Music builds around silence. Sports call time-outs. Formal meals often have sorbets, to refresh the palate before the next course. Behind the Sabbath, our holidays and our vacations from the job is the notion that all work includes rest. Rest is not escape, but essential to the high calling of our daily work."

―――――

STUDY
Our modern lives are incredibly busy. And often the busyness, the weight of the to-do list, the demands of life seem to have the loudest voice. But there is a Voice, His voice, who speaks rest to the weary.

Charles Spurgeon said, "Repose is as needful to the mind as sleep to the body ... If we do not rest, we shall break down. Even the earth must lie fallow and have her Sabbaths, and so must we. Jesus said, 'Come apart and rest awhile.'" And if we do not "come apart," we will come apart indeed!

"The number one enemy of Christian spiritual formation today is exhaustion," writes James Bryan Smith in *The Good and Beautiful God*. "Sleep is an act of surrender. It is a declaration of trust. It is admitting to God that we are not God (who never sleeps), and that is good news."

Our culture says work, work, work then collapse on the weekend only to begin the process all over again. Work becomes all-encompassing (toil) and rest becomes mindless escape (leisure). Neither of these patterns is true to God's design for us. He calls us to work differently and also to rest differently. Our work is to be done sacredly, to bring greater good and transformation in our world and to serve others and give Him glory. Our rest is actually an act of faith as we trust in Him while we cease from activity. True rest is restorative and should anchor and fuel our work. If we follow His rhythm of working from a place of rest, then work and rest both become deeply soul-satisfying.

God created man on the sixth day (Genesis 1:24-2:3) and then He rested. So the first thing that man did with God was rest. Then he worked. This is the pattern that we were created for. This counter-cultural rhythm that marks our lives is working from a place of rest instead of working and then resting. Rest is where we begin, NOT end.

Jesus explained this rhythm in the concept of abiding and growing (John 15:4-5). We grow from a place of abiding, resting, remaining in Him. This beautiful pattern roots us in Jesus and releases us from self-effort, the try-hard life.

The Church stands apart from the culture of our world as a people of rest. We need daily rest in prayer and the Word, a time of devotion or quiet time. Jesus modeled spiritual rest for us (Mark 1:35). He also modeled physical rest. Jesus took a nap in a boat in the middle of a storm (Mark 4:35-41). He unapologetically slept when His body needed it.

Jesus doesn't just offer rest. He demonstrates that it is a necessity, not a luxury. Resting is actually an act of worship, not a sign of laziness. And with great compassion He invites us to come in our weariness and receive rest, to abide in Him and then work from a place of rest.

READ
Isaiah 55:1-3a, Matthew 11:28-30

HEAD

Look at the repeated verbs in Isaiah 55:1-3a. What is God inviting you to do? How will you respond?

HEART

Read Matthew 11:28-30 in the Message translation. Ask the Spirit to reveal any disorder in your work and rest life. Is rest difficult for you? Consider the counterclockwise rhythm, an unforced rhythm of grace. Are your work and rest patterns in step with Jesus in this life-giving rhythm?

Think back to your family of origin. What patterns of work and rest did you see modeled? How did this shape you?

HANDS

Look at your calendar. Schedule times of rest with the Lord daily and weekly.

Share with one another how you rest.

A SPIRITUAL EXERCISE

Take a moment to enter into this painting *Noonday Rest* by Vincent Van Gogh and the following poem:

Noonday Rest
Marilyn Chandler McEntyre

To rest before the sheaves are bound,
toss the scythes aside, bare the feet and sink
into the nearest haystack, release
the undone task and consent to sleep
while the brightest hour burns an arc
across its stretch of sky;
this is the body's prayer, mid-day angelus
whispered in mingled breath while the limbs
stretch in thanksgiving and the body turns
toward the beloved.

This is the prayer of trust;
what's left undone will wait. The unattended
child, the uncut acre, cracked wheel, broken
fence that are the occupations of waking mind
soften into shadow in the semi-darkness
of dream. All shall be well. Little depends on us.
The turning world is held and borne in love.
We give good measure in our toil and, meet and right,
obey the body when it calls us to rest.

Now find a spot to rest. How has God spoken to you through the painting and poem? Be still and pay attention to anything He might be bringing to the surface.

Is it difficult for you to rest? Why? Read Zephaniah 3:17. Picture Him now, quieting you. Feel His love, His delight resting on you. Hear Him singing over you as you rest, a sweet lullaby of His care. Release to Him all that burdens you. Close your eyes in trust. Sleep, dear child of God.

LECTIO DIVINA
Mark 4:35-41

MEMORY VERSE
Matthew 11:28-29

"Come to me, all you who are weary and burdened, and I will give you rest. Take my yoke upon you and learn from me, for I am gentle and humble in heart, and you will find rest for your souls."

THE INVITATIONS OF JESUS

MISSION

- SERVE
- GIVE
- GO

Jesus invites us to serve because He first served us through His radical love so that we can serve others within the church and then to the least of these.

STORY
a true story of William Wilberforce

In the late 1700s, English traders were raiding the African coast on the Gulf of Guinea, capturing between 35,000 and 50,000 Africans a year. The British economy was so dependent on slave trade that many excused it as a necessary evil and thought it could never change. William Wilberforce was one of those who thought he could end the evil of slavery. Wilberforce grew up in a prominent family with much wealth and political aspirations. But he then felt purposeless and experienced a period of intense sorrow. In that place, he had a spiritual rebirth. He initially thought he would dedicate his life to the church but soon realized the providence of his public position to end slavery and the reformation of society.

With the eyes of Jesus, he was seeing the brokenness of the world and responding to the slave trade, the poor, child labor abuses, terrible working conditions, single mothers, orphans and juvenile delinquents. He relentlessly introduced resolutions and bills against the slave trade. From 1789 to 1806, all of his anti-slavery efforts were defeated by the slave trade interest and political fear. And then finally in 1807, Parliament abolished the slave trade in the British Empire. Three days prior to Wilberforce's death in 1833, he heard the emancipation bill, which abolished all slavery, had been passed.

STUDY

War, famine, human trafficking, refugees, sexual assault, poverty, racial discrimination ... the list is endless and the needs daunting. We are tempted to say it is too big for us or we don't care because we have become desensitized to the brokenness of this world. With our busy schedules and demands, these needs often feel distant and we don't know how to respond. But God responds. He has been responding from the beginning of time bringing the good, the true and the beautiful where there was empty darkness.

He first responds to the brokenness of our souls. His love, through Jesus' death and resurrection on the cross was the remedy for our brokenness. He gave life and meaning to love: "This is how we know what love is: Jesus Christ laid down his life for us. And we ought to lay down our lives for our brothers and sisters" (1 John 3:16).

Our response is to first receive His love and be rescued and restored by it. Then, as He serves us through His love, we serve others by His love. We are a part of His rescue and restoration to our lost and broken world. So, what does that look like? For Jesus, we see Him providing wine at a party, feeding the hungry, healing the leper, saving the adulterous woman, hanging out with the despised and outcast, washing the disciples' feet and finally giving His life for all. For us, it should reverberate out in concentric circles. Starting with our family, friends and co-workers, to our city and country and then to the world. Practically, it could look like bringing a meal to someone in need, listening to and praying with a friend who is hurting, fixing a house for a single mother or widow, volunteering with a mission partner or serving internationally in missions. The important thing is to be led by the Holy Spirit so that we might have the eyes to see, the heart to respond and the faith to act. The Holy Spirit speaks to us through thoughts, ideas, nudges, dreams and sometimes even words. But remember that it all should be tested by Scripture and submitted to the wisdom of the church community. And as we serve, remember the words of Jesus, "I tell you the truth, whatever you did for one of the least of these brothers and sisters of mine, you did for me" (Matthew 25:40).

READ
John 13:1-17, 31-35, Isaiah 58:5-8

HEAD
In John 13, Jesus showed them the "full extent of his love" by washing the disciples' feet. What was significant about Jesus washing their feet? Why did Jesus call "love one another" a new command?

In Isaiah 58, we are given a picture of what "true fasting" looks like. "Fasting" is to abstain from food or drink for a period of time to turn our hearts towards God in reliance on Him for strength. This picture of "true fasting" speaks to the heart of God. What struck you about this picture? What does it say is at the core of God's heart?

HEART

Jesus says in John 13:35, "By this all men will know that you are my disciples, if you love one another." If a good friend or spouse was given one word to describe your life, would they say "love"? If not, what?

How well does your heart align with God's heart as depicted in Isaiah 58? If it is not aligned, why is that so?

HANDS

Watch the movie *Amazing Grace* directed by Michael Apted.

Fasting in Scripture is often a reflection of devotion and righteousness. If Isaiah 58 is a picture of "true fasting," what should our devotion and righteousness look like? What could we specifically do to respond to the brokenness of the world around us?

If you are a parent, are there opportunities to serve together as a family (feeding the homeless, making a meal for someone in need, child sponsorship, etc.)?

SPIRITUAL EXERCISE

For the rest of the week, start each day with the following prayer, "Lord, give me the eyes today to see the brokenness of this world, the heart to respond and the faith to act." At the end of the week, get together with a friend and share how you saw God show up.

LECTIO DIVINA

John 13:1-17

MEMORY VERSE

Mark 10:45

"For even the Son of Man did not come to be served, but to serve, and to give his life as a ransom for many."

. . . .

Jesus invites and frees us to live joyfully generous lives for his Kingdom.

STORY
a true story from The Generous Giving Conference, GenerousGiving.org

Scott and Kristen Lewis, with their four children, were a typical American family except that their hearts were captured by Jesus Christ, and they desired to serve him on the mission field. Scott and Kristen went on a short-term mission trip to Albania with Cru to show the *Jesus Film*. After sharing their testimonies, they were approached by a high school girl, who had surrendered her life to Jesus Christ. She was begging them to come again to Albania and tell all her friends about God. They returned home to Sacramento with the goal of selling their tool business and joining Cru in Albania. They had no idea what the Lord had planned for them.

When their deal to sell their business collapsed at the last minute, they decided to liquidate and go anyway. Scott was awakened in the night with a strong impression from the Lord that they were to stay put. While they didn't understand, they obeyed.

Months later they met Bill Bright and Dave Hannah, who challenged them to become part of "History's Handful," a group of 1,200 people giving $1 million each to distribute the *Jesus Film* to every people group. While they thought it was crazy, they both sensed the Lord calling them to make the commitment although they had no idea where that much money would come from. At the time, they were already committed to generously giving $17,000/year, which was 35% of their income. Bill Bright challenged them to make $50,000 their goal for the next year and see what the Lord did with their business.

At the end of the next year, they were far from reaching their goal of $50,000. However, they received an unlikely call about a certain machine at the last moment. That deal enabled them to reach their goal of giving $50,000 to the mission. By the end of the next year [the following year] they had the $50,000, but it was all of the profit for the business. After wrestling with whether to give away all their profit, they gave it away. The next day, they did $65,000 in sales, which included $27,000 profit. This was the exact amount they needed to fulfill their goal of $50,000. In a single day, they had replenished their business capital.

The Lord began to bless their business, and the next year they set a goal of giving $100,000 to the mission. By the end of the year, they had given away $57,000 and had the remaining $43,000 in the bank. After wrestling with their fear of clearing out their bank account, they gave the $43,000 to the mission. From that day forward, the Lord increasingly blessed their business financially. They acquired the habit of draining their business account at the end of every year and giving the money to the mission.

At the time they were interviewed, they had given away a total of $734,000 including $175,000 in the last year. They were well on their way to reaching their goal of giving away $1 million - beyond their wildest dreams! They thought they were going to serve the Lord by moving to Albania, but the Lord had other plans. He had a paradigm shift for them. Instead of sending them to Albania, He had blessed them with the skills to run a business for the purpose of funding His Kingdom priorities. There was another paradigm shift needed too. They learned they could not out-give God! Throughout this adventure, they had experienced the overflowing joy of living as friends and allies with the Lord in His Kingdom mission.

STUDY

The story of the Lewis family is both challenging and exciting. It also illustrates a truth taught throughout the Bible: the God and Father of our Lord Jesus Christ is the most joyfully generous Person in the universe. After all, He demonstrated His generosity by giving His Son Jesus Christ to be our crucified and risen Savior (John 3:16). Jesus revealed this same generosity by becoming poor so that we might have the treasure of the King and His Kingdom (2 Corinthians 8:9).

Moreover, the Lord calls us to share in His joy by living generously towards His Kingdom priorities. Throughout the Bible, we are taught of the great joy and blessing in giving from a cheerful heart transformed by grace. Jesus Himself taught, "It is more blessed to give than receive" (Acts 20:35). Clearly to be a disciple of King Jesus is to be transformed into a joyfully generous person with all that we have including our time, talent and treasure.

Many of us find it easier to be generous with our time and talent than with our treasure. Why is that? Perhaps we've never realized that all we have really belongs to the Lord, and we are His managers (Psalm 24:1, Matthew 25:14-30). In a materialistic, consumer culture like ours, we can be tempted to consume more and more (Luke 12:13-21). It's easy to forget that we will ultimately give an account to the Lord for how we used the time, talent and treasure He entrusted to us (Romans 14:12, 1 Corinthians 4:2, 2 Corinthians 5:9-10).

While all of this may be true of us, we almost certainly wrestle with the fear that if we give too much away, we will not have enough to live on. Every desire to be financially generous may have a corresponding impulse of fear. This is normal because fear and faith usually go together. Anytime we are responding to the Lord's invitation to grow in our faith, we are likely to battle a corresponding fear.

In His wisdom, the Lord has taken our fear into account. He has set up the economics of His Kingdom to work in our favor when we reject fear in favor of generosity. Jesus addresses this fear directly in His famous sermon (Matthew 6:19-34). We see Jesus appealing to our motive for the best investments (v. 19-21), appealing to us to see clearly with an eternal perspective (v. 22-23) and saying that money makes a great tool but a lousy god (v. 24). Jesus next addresses our fear that if we are generous, we will lack what we need (v. 25-34). Jesus introduces us to a promise of God: if we make God's Kingdom our priority, He will provide what we need to live. If we believe He really is in charge of the world's economy, then we can trust Him to take care of us while we are giving to His Kingdom priorities. Faith overcomes fear.

Paul addresses this same promise in 2 Corinthians 8-9. After commending the poor Macedonian Christians for their generosity, he exhorts the Corinthian Christians to join them (2 Corinthians 8:1-15). Paul addresses their fear of giving by teaching the spiritual law of the harvest (2 Corinthians 9:6-15). If a farmer wants a crop, he must sow his seed. In the same way, the Lord has set up the economics of the Kingdom to reward those who are financially generous. We may fear we don't have enough money to be generous, but that's like thinking we can't risk sowing seed in a field for a crop.

When we give from a cheerful heart transformed by grace, the Lord will return to us more than we give. This is not, as the prosperity gospel proponents contend, a way to get materially rich. Instead, it's the Lord's way of addressing our fear that if we are generous toward His priorities, we will lack what we need. His purpose in blessing us is so that we can joyfully partner with Him (2 Corinthians 9:10-11).

"For many believers, cheerful giving has become fearful giving. We are not opposed to supporting God's kingdom with our resources. And we're not really greedy. But we are concerned. We're concerned that if we don't look after our own needs first, they might not get looked after at all.

Yet the testimony of Scripture, together with the experiences of millions of believers, sends a resounding response to our concerns. Any fear associated with giving to God's kingdom is irrational. It's on par with a farmer who, out of fear of losing his seed, refuses to plant his fields. The principle of sowing and reaping applies to our finances. Those who sow generously can expect to reap generously and receive a bountiful return.

God's nature is to replenish the stores of those who strive to be faithful conduits for His Kingdom work. When you participate with God in His mission, you can trust Him to reward you abundantly for every good deed. When you begin to view your wealth from God's perspective, you'll see that the thing to fear isn't giving away too much, but sowing too little." - Andy Stanley, Fields of Gold

READ
2 Corinthians 8- 9

HEAD
Paul uses the Macedonian Christians' generosity to motivate the Corinthian Christians to keep their pledge to help the Jerusalem Christians (8:1-15). He challenges them to "see that you excel in this grace of giving" (8:7). What are the marks of transforming grace in the Macedonian Christians?

Paul applies the principle of sowing and reaping (law of the harvest) to motivate the Corinthian Christians (9:6-11). What exactly does Paul promise those who are financially generous towards the Lord's priorities?

What is the standard of giving Paul recommends?

HEART

What is your primary motivation when you give to ministries? Would you describe yourself as a cheerful giver (2 Corinthians 9:7)?

What do you consider to be generous giving? Does it change your view to consider that all your money really belongs to the Lord and He has entrusted it to you as His manager?

What are the fears you have about financial giving? How are those fears addressed by Jesus and Paul?

HANDS

Do you currently have a specific plan for how you give to your local church and other Kingdom ministries? If not, what are you ready to do? If so, are you willing to consider how you might trust the Lord's law of sowing and reaping to increase your giving?

SPIRITUAL EXERCISE

Take time to read and pray over the following biblical principles of financial stewardship (the four Ps):

1. Priority giving = of all the items in your monthly budget, the Lord's share comes first. We give to Him before we pay bills or spend money on ourselves (1 Corinthians 16:2, Proverbs 3:9-10).
2. Percentage giving = you decide on a percentage of your income you will give regularly regardless of your emotions or circumstances (1 Corinthians 16:2, Deuteronomy 16:10, 16-17). How much can you give cheerfully and not reluctantly (2 Corinthians 9:7)?
3. Progressive giving = can you decide you want to grow in generosity and increase your giving over time? Perhaps you can slowly increase the percentage you give. Perhaps you determine to live at a set standard of living and give everything over that amount.
4. Prompted giving = you are sensitive to the Lord's promptings to give to special occasions (1 John 3:17). This is over and above your regular giving.

Read *Fields of Gold* by Andy Stanley or *The Treasure Principle* by Randy Alcorn to grow in your theology of financial stewardship. They are both short and easy to read.

LECTIO DIVINA
Luke 12:13-26

MEMORY VERSE
2 Corinthians 9:6-8

"Remember this: Whoever sows sparingly will also reap sparingly, and whoever sows generously will also reap generously. Each man should give what he has decided in his heart to give, not reluctantly or under compulsion, for God loves a cheerful giver. And God is able to make all grace abound to you, so that in all things at all times, having all that you need, you will abound in every good work."

. . . .

Jesus invites us to "GO" on mission with Him, empowered by the Holy Spirit, rescuing and restoring our lost and broken world back to God.

STORY
a true story of one of the Church's pioneering missionaries

In 1853, Hudson Taylor, at the age of 21, set sail from England on a little three-masted clipper to serve as a missionary in China. As a teenager he experienced a spiritual birth that left him with a passionate burden for the souls of China. He once said, "China is not to be won for Christ by quiet, ease-loving men and women … the stamp of men and women we need is such as will put Jesus, China [and] souls first and foremost in everything and at every time - even life itself must be secondary." And so he gave his life for the people of China.

He had studied medicine and treated many patients as a way to serve the people and preach the gospel. He soon founded a new mission that focused on taking the gospel to the interior called, 'China Inland Missions' (now serving as OMF International). Their organization distinctions were that their missionaries would not have guaranteed salaries, nor could they appeal for funds. They would simply trust God to supply their needs. Furthermore, their missionaries would adopt Chinese dress and push the gospel into the interior of China. Hudson Taylor was also known for bold policies such as having unmarried women serving in the interior. Through missionaries like Hudson Taylor and many others in China, the seed of the gospel has taken root and now the church in China numbers around 150 million believers. And they too are now sending out missionaries to other areas where people have never heard the Gospel.

STUDY
———

"Missions exist because worship doesn't." - John Piper

———

God's mission flows from God's heart to our lost and broken world. As God calls us to the ways of Jesus, missions are the overflow of discipleship. It does not start with us, it starts with God. We observe this even from the first pages of Scripture. God created and it was good. God brought light, order, beauty and life where there was empty darkness. When Adam and Eve succumbed to the temptation of Satan, all of creation fell. But God did not give up on His creation. He sent His Son, Jesus, as our rescue and restoration from sin and brokenness. He now calls us to "GO" and be part of His mission of rescue and restoration to our lost and broken world.

So, is God's mission providing clean drinking water to desolate areas, fighting against human trafficking, orphan care, witnessing to our neighbor, preaching the gospel to people who have never heard? The answer is yes. But the heart and priority of mission is the rescue of lost people under the penalty and power of sin. Even Jesus said, "For the Son of Man came to seek and to save what was lost" (Luke 19:10); or Jesus' words when He healed the paralytic, "But that you may know that the Son of Man has authority on earth to forgive sins … I tell you, get up, take your mat and go home" (Luke 5:24). Jesus had compassion for the paralytic's physical state but was actually more concerned about the paralytic's spiritual state. The greatest brokenness of humanity is our sin. Physical brokenness does not separate us from God, sin does. Jesus rescues people from the bondage and death sentence of sin, and He also restores them to greater wholeness. This is seen when Jesus started His ministry by reading from the prophet Isaiah, "The Spirit of the Lord is on me, because he has anointed me to preach good news to the poor. He has sent me to proclaim freedom for the prisoners and recovery of sight for the blind, to release the oppressed, to proclaim the year of the Lord's favor" (Luke 4:18-19).

Let us be reminded that as we "GO" to make disciples, Jesus first spoke these words to the disciples and some even doubted (Matthew 28:17). Just as Jesus met them where they were, He meets us where we are. The Great Commission is not based on our expertise or boldness, but rather on His authority and power. As Jesus said, "All authority in heaven and on earth has been given to me". And from His authority and power, out of the overflow of His heart, we tell others about the hope, love and salvation that is in Jesus.

READ
Luke 10:1-17, Matthew 28:16-20

HEAD

When Jesus sent off the disciples in twos, what did he tell them to do? Why was it important for them to heal the sick?

What does a "man of peace" look like in our day and age?

In the Matthew passage, with what authority do we "GO"? What does that tangibly look like for you?

HEART

When you think of being on mission with God, what are your fears or hesitations?

The disciples returned with joy as they saw God powerfully at work. How have you experienced joy in the mission of God?

HANDS

For the next year, pray about a mission opportunity you can partner with such as Family Promise, Day of Champions with Behind the Walls Ministry, Alternatives Pregnancy Center, Restoration Outreach Programs, Tijuana, Albania, Kenya, India, etc.

Start praying for a friend, co-worker or neighbor who does not know Jesus. Use the Spiritual Exercise below to help.

SPIRITUAL EXERCISE

This week start each morning by praying, "Lord, break my heart for those who are lost and broken. Help me to see what you are doing in peoples' lives and give me the boldness to speak of your hope, love and salvation to them." Use the "Prayer, Care, Share" bookmark included in Appendix J. Who can you be praying for, caring for and sharing with? Maybe it is a family member, friend, co-worker or neighbor. Also, read Appendix K to learn more about the remaining task of missions.

LECTIO DIVINA
Matthew 28:16-20

MEMORY VERSE
Matthew 28:18-20

"Then Jesus came to them and said, "All authority in heaven and on earth has been given to me. Therefore, go and make disciples of all nations, baptizing them in the name of the Father and of the Son and of the Holy Spirit, and teaching them to obey everything I have commanded you. And surely I am with you always, to the very end of the age."

APPENDICES

- APPENDICES A - K
- LEADER'S GUIDE
- AUTHORS' BOOK RECOMMENDATIONS

Appendix A

· ·

——• LECTIO DIVINA
Contemplative Bible Reading

 "Blessed is the man who does not walk in the counsel of the wicked ... But his delight is in the law of the Lord, and on His law he meditates day and night." Psalm 1:1-2

Contrary to our more common cognitive and analytical approach of studying Scripture, contemplative reading or Bible meditation is a slower approach that seeks to hear the Lord's Word to us with our hearts. It is the difference between the informational and formational reading of Scripture.

Jesus continually called His disciples to listen at the heart level - "He who has ears to hear, let him hear" (Matthew 11:15, 13:9-17, 43). In *The Practice of Prayer*, Robert Warren wisely says, "... truly to hear, and in listening to obey, is at the heart of knowing God. ... This knowing and being known takes place when God's Word so penetrates our innermost being that we become what we hear. We are transformed into God's likeness. ... This is how intimacy with God takes place."

One of the oldest and best ways of reading Scripture is called by its Latin name, *Lectio Divina*, which means "divine reading" or "spiritual reading." It consists of a four-part movement, beginning with the text and ending in prayer. The goal is to allow the Lord to speak a word to you through the text.

Step One: Reading/Listening
Prepare to read by quieting yourself (centering). You will need to sit upright in a chair; practice taking deep breaths to slow yourself down. Practice the Lord's Presence by reminding yourself that He is with you at this very moment. Some find it helpful to set an empty chair in front of them and imagine Jesus sitting there.

Read aloud a short passage of Scripture. As you read, listen for a word or phrase that speaks to you. You may have to read the passage several times slowly. What is the Spirit drawing your attention to? You are listening for the "word within the word," such as a key phrase or promise.

Note: Each person's prayer relationship with the Lord is unique. In some, the imaginative faculty is more developed and active. Some may find it helpful to use their imaginations to enter into the scene, seeing and hearing the persons, imagining the touch and smells. Others may rely more on their intuition by savoring the truth or insight inherent in the passage. Whatever our approach to prayer, a basic principle applies: "Pray as you can, not as you can't!"

Step Two: Meditating

Repeat aloud the word or phrase to which you are drawn. Here, you are allowing the word or phrase to sink into your heart. Make connections between it and your life. What is the Spirit saying to you by means of this word or phrase?

Step Three: Praying

What is the Spirit leading you to pray? Now take these thoughts and offer them back to God in prayer, giving thanks, asking for guidance or forgiveness and resting in God's love.

Step Four: Contemplating

This is resting in God's Presence. We move from the activity of prayer to the stillness of contemplation. Stay open to God, listen to Him. Remain in peace and silence before God. You are allowing the text to work its way into the deepest part of your being. You are savoring an encounter. How is God revealing Himself to you? It is helpful to record your thoughts in a journal.

———

"The gospel is not a doctrine of the tongue, but of life. It cannot be grasped by reason and memory only, but it is fully understood when it possesses the whole soul, and penetrates to the inner recesses of the heart." - John Calvin

———

———

"In our meditation we ponder the chosen text on the strength of the promise that it has something utterly personal to say to us for this day and for our Christian life, that it is not only God's Word for the Church, but also God's Word for us individually. We expose ourselves to the specific word until it addresses us personally. And when we do this, we are doing no more than the simplest, untutored Christian does every day; we read God's Word as God's Word for us." - Dietrich Bonhoeffer, Life Together

———

Appendix B

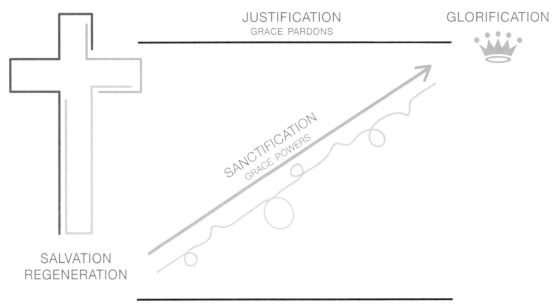

This diagram illustrates theological realities of our faith. We receive salvation through the regeneration (rebirth) of the Spirit and no longer live life dead in our sin and relationally broken with God. We are fully justified (forgiven and made relationally right) with God through His grace pardoning our sin. Our new life of sanctification (being progressively made like Jesus) begins, and the power of His grace through the indwelling of the Holy Spirit transforms us. The blue line indicates how God sees our growth. He views us through the completed work of Christ, as expressed in 2 Corinthians 5:17, "Therefore, if anyone is in Christ, he is a new creation; the old has gone, the new has come!" But we experience the reality of our growth as expressed in the green line. These are the paradoxical realities of sanctification. And finally, at our physical death we will be fully transformed by His glory and into His glory to live joyfully and love Him forever.

Appendix C

....

──• BARRIERS TO INTIMACY WITH GOD: Sin, Wounds and Warfare

God. What must God be like? He keeps every living creature breathing. He spins the stars and makes them burn. Everything beautiful you have ever seen - mountain streams sparkling in the sunlight, fawns bouncing through meadows, poppies of every color dancing in the spring breeze, glittering pure white snow - is an artistic expression of His glory, a stroke from His creation brush. And, He is love (1 John 4:8). What kind of love must such a being possess? Infinite love. Faithful love. Joyous love. Unfading, undying love. Redeeming love. Sacrificial love. Every kind of human love we have witnessed, experienced or longed for is a dim reflection of His great heart: He is a Trinity - a pulsing, living community of divine love.

And this great, glorious, good being has invited us to know Him: "And this is eternal life, that they know you, the only true God" (John 17:3). In fact, He has invited us *into* Himself (John 17:21).

So why do we struggle to find joy in God, to find comfort in His love?

We all have barriers to intimacy with God in our hearts: sin, wounds and warfare swirl together and solidify in our souls to create a wall between our hearts and God's heart. This wall keeps God's love, joy and hope from being poured into us. It keeps us from receiving His love, from loving Him back and from loving others as He does.

──• SIN

We are born with a sin nature (Psalm 51:5), a base-level mistrust of and antipathy toward God. J.I. Packer says we are all infected with an "irrational anti-God syndrome." It makes us suspicious toward God, inclines us not to trust Him and tempts us to blame Him for everything we can.

As we go through life, our sin nature prompts us to ignore God's commands and choose sinful ways to get what we think we need for happiness or wellbeing. Doing this, we sear our consciences (1 Timothy 4:2). We mistrust God and disbelieve that He has good things for us, so we disobey Him. Then we feel guilty, and this makes us angry or ashamed, increasing our desire to keep away from God. The wall grows.

On top of this, other people sin against us, wounding our hearts.

⟶• WOUNDS

We were created for perfect love, but no one on earth loves perfectly. For this reason, each one of us is wounded in the very relationships that also nurture and bless us. Additionally, some people in our lives have wantonly chosen to wound us or rob us of precious things to satisfy their own sinful desires.

When we are wounded, we try to make sense of what happened to us. Because of our innate distrust of God, we often create false explanations: God is cruel; God doesn't care; I'm unlovable; God doesn't even exist; There's something wrong with me.

We also choose to nurture bitterness and anger toward those that have hurt us and toward God Himself.

Our pain, our false beliefs and our anger add cement to the wall between God's heart and ours.

⟶• WARFARE

On top of this, we have an evil, merciless and deadly enemy: Satan. He hates us because God loves us and because we bear His image. Satan's goal is to destroy us. He wants us to despise ourselves, to hate God and to hurt other people. He gets a foothold in our lives in numerous ways: sin, trauma, family lines and occult activities.

When we repeatedly engage in a sinful thought pattern or behavior, it's as if we wear down our immune system to demonic oppression. Eventually we can be 'infected' with a spiritually-oppressive spirit related to our chosen sin. These might be spirits of anger, lust, greed, pride or any form of addiction.

Our enemy doesn't play fair, and he will capitalize on our wounds, or the traumatic events in our lives, to prey upon us. Car accidents, illnesses, the loss of a loved one or someone's sin against us can create an opening for him to tell us lies and oppress us. This kind of oppression might come from spirits of shame, fear, anxiety or self-hatred.

Demons also access family lines, possibly through the wounds our families give us, and sinful patterns or struggles can be passed to us through our families.

Lastly, any kind of occult involvement - Ouija boards, tarot cards, seances, reciting spells or curses, occult objects - can open us up to powerful occult spirits.

Demonic or satanic oppression in our lives always works against intimacy with God. God loves us and is good. Satan wants us to believe we are bad and God is worse. He will always work to support the wall between God's heart and ours.

→ TEARING DOWN THE WALL BETWEEN GOD'S HEART AND OURS

Most of the tools you need to tear down the wall and draw nearer to God you will find in this guide: community, spiritual disciplines, mentoring, worship and service. You are on your way! Sometimes, however, we need special help to overcome certain areas of sin, deep wounds or troublesome warfare. This may come in the form of Intensive Healing Prayer. (See Appendix I for more information.)

Appendix D

....

→ BIBLE STUDY BASICS

Because the Bible is God's Word in human words, it must be read with both our hearts and minds. Therefore, the key to reading and studying the Bible is to approach Scripture in a posture of humility, prayer and serious attentiveness to the words recorded. This is the only way to hear the Lord's Word to us (Proverbs 2:1-5). While there are definite guidelines for correctly understanding the Bible, they are not a substitute for prayerfully relying on the Holy Spirit to give you revelation and understanding (John 16:13-15, 1 Corinthians 2:6-16).

→ THREE STAGES OF INDUCTIVE BIBLE STUDY

There are three steps in inductive Bible study: (1) Observing and reading the text carefully with the question, "What does the passage actually say?; (2) Interpretation - What was the author's intended meaning?; and (3) Application - How does this passage apply to me/us?

I.   Observation - What does the passage actually say?

Read with a purpose, i.e., ask investigative questions:

·   *Who wrote it? Who is it written to?*
·   *Who is there? What is the setting?*
·   *What are they doing? What is happening?*
·   *How are they described?*
·   *Are there repeating words/phrases?*
·   *Are there contrasts or connections between ideas, words or people?*

II. Interpretation - What was the author's intended meaning?

Each biblical passage had an objective meaning intended by its author for the original audience. Sometimes, the New Testament will provide a more nuanced meaning than the original Old Testament author or editor intended. This is because the Holy Spirit (the ultimate author) had a deeper intention than the human author knew.

There are certain principles of biblical interpretation that must be followed for an accurate understanding of Scripture. All these principles are designed to help us understand the author's intended meaning to his original audience (this process is called "exegesis"). The following are sound principles of biblical interpretation:[i]

a. Identify the type/genre of literature.

The Bible is both a single book and a library of 66 books. It was written by at least 40 different human authors over a period of 1,500 years. The oldest book is believed to have been written about 1400 BC or earlier. The last book was written about 100 AD. The Bible was written in Hebrew (OT) and Greek (NT).

The Bible includes many different types or genres of literature. A genre of literature is a group of texts that share similarity in context, tone and structure. The Bible consists of the following genres of literature: historical narrative, law codes, poetry, wisdom, prophecy, gospels, parables, epistles and apocalyptic. Each genre of biblical literature is read differently.[ii]

b. Identify the historical and cultural context.

The Bible is not a transcultural document. It is both divine and human. The Bible is fully the Word of God in human words. It is God's Word which has taken a particular human form in a particular time and culture. The Lord inspired His Words in the genres of the day using native literary conventions. This means:

1. Each document in the Bible is conditioned by the language, time and culture in which it was originally written.
2. The Lord expressed His Word through the vocabulary and thought patterns of the original authors.
3. We must seek to understand, as much as possible, the original author and when and why the literature was written.
4. The Lord's Word to us was first His Word to them.
5. Most of the time this means consulting some outside help such as a Bible Dictionary or commentary.

c. **Read Scripture in its literary context.**

This principle arises from the truth that words have meaning only in context. Context gives meaning to a specific word, phrase or sentence. Context can be expanded into paragraphs, chapters, books, etc. These various levels of context may be envisioned as a series of concentric circles moving out from the specific passage:

1. the immediate context = the words, sentences and paragraphs that lead up to and follow the passage;
2. the chapters of the particular book;
3. the Old or New Testament;
4. the Canon of the Bible.

d. **Consider the grammar and structure within the passage.**

We need to see how the author's thought flows; therefore, we look for connectors, verb tenses and noun modifiers. We also must seek to understand the meaning of a key word or phrase used by the author.

e. **Always seek the full counsel of Scripture.**

While the Bible is an anthology of many books, it is also one Book. The Bible has many stories to tell, but they all contribute to a single Story. To grasp the full counsel of Scripture, we need to study the themes and analogies that stretch from Genesis to Revelation. Then, when we read any one passage, we will be able to understand its place in the larger Story. This is particularly important when reading the Old Testament, which pointed to Jesus and finds its ultimate meaning in Jesus Christ (see Luke 24:25-27, 44).

Scripture teaches us the principle of progressive revelation. Therefore, we must consider the New Testament's development of a particular theme or command found in the Old Testament. For example, some of the Lord's commands for His people have changed from one phase of redemptive history to another, i.e., Old Testament sacrificial laws are fulfilled in Christ. Similarly, laws separating clean and unclean animals or persons are no longer in effect. In order to determine how a particular verse of Scripture must be applied to our lives, we must locate it within the redemptive-historical context of the Bible. The New Testament fulfills and modifies the Old Testament.

The Holy Spirit is the divine Author who moved human authors to write exactly what God intended to be written. Because God is its primary Author, there is an organic unity to Scripture. This organic unity implies that the ultimate meaning of any part of Scripture, such as a verse or book, is determined by its place in the whole. Different texts speak to the same issues, thus modifying and reinforcing each other as they present a unified message. The organic structure of Scripture is called the "analogy of Scripture" or the "analogy of faith."

Because Scripture is ultimately the work of the Holy Spirit, we believe that Scripture will never contradict Scripture. Therefore, clear passages take priority over unclear passages. Doctrine and moral teachings should not be based on obscure passages, but on clear and repeated teachings. Therefore, we must be careful not to "proof-text" Scripture by taking verses out of their specific context or the larger context of the canon of Scripture.

III. Application - How does this passage apply to me/us?

The goal of application is to hear God's Word to us here and now (this process is called "hermeneutics"). Here is the crucial difference between our reading and studying of Scripture being transformative instead of merely informative. Without a **concrete** and **specific** application, it is too easy to be like the "man who looks at his face in a mirror and, after looking at himself, goes away and immediately forgets what he looks like" (James 1:23-24). What's the difference? One merely listens to the Word while the other actually obeys it.

2 Timothy 3:16-17 gives us the *how* of application (teaching, rebuking, correcting and training in righteousness). Therefore, our response to what we read must be a response of humble and tenacious obedience. A balanced response would include both our encouragement and exhortation, attitude and action, healing and repentance.

Basic application questions:

a. Is there a truth to embrace … about the Lord … about me?
b. Is there an attitude to assume?
c. Is there an example to follow or avoid?
d. Is there a command to obey?
e. Is there a sin to confess?
f. Is there a promise to embrace?
g. Is there an encouragement to receive?
h. Is there a way to pray?
i. Are there new insights or difficulties to explore further?

Note: It may be necessary to ask additional questions about the main teaching of the passage (especially if it is in the Old Testament): Does the passage teach something that applies only to a specific people? To a cultural problem of its day? To a certain time in history? We must be careful that we don't take a cultural standard and make it apply as an eternal standard for all times and places.

➔ RECOMMENDED RESOURCES

1. *How to Read the Bible Book by Book*, Gordon Fee & Doug Stuart (Zondervan, 2002)
2. *Reading the Bible With Heart & Mind*, Tremper Longman III (NavPress 1997)
3. *How to Read the Bible through the Jesus Lens*, Michael Williams (Zondervan 2012)
4. *Making Sense of the Old Testament - Three Crucial Questions*, Tremper Longman III (Baker Books 1998)
5. *How to Read the Bible For All Its Worth*, Gordon Fee & Douglas Stuart (Zondervan, 1982)

It should be noted that everyone follows certain principles of interpreting the Bible, i.e., methods of understanding Scripture and applying it to their lives. It is too simplistic to say there are simply "Bible believing" Christians who take the Bible at face value whereas others use certain "man-made" rules. We all use methods for understanding the meaning of Scripture and applying it to our lives.

For a basic discussion of the various types of biblical literature and their principles of interpretation, see *Reading the Bible With Heart & Mind by Tremper Longman III (NavPress 1997)*. For an even more detailed description, see *How to Read the Bible For All Its Worth by Gordon Fee & Douglas Stuart (Zondervan 1982)*.

Appendix E

. . . .

—• A CONTEMPLATIVE LORD'S PRAYER

"Our Father" *Think of a moment where you experienced or can imagine the tender love of a father. Now, bask in that feeling as an outpouring of the love of your Heavenly Father. "He loves you, because He loves you, because He loves you ..."*

"Hallowed be your name." *Hallowed means holy, sacred and revered. Imagine God as the creator of the Universe, holy and exalted, worthy to be praised. Praise Him.*

"Your kingdom come, your will be done on earth as it is in heaven." *God's kingdom is righteousness, peace and joy in the Holy Spirit (Romans 14:17). Think through what you might be doing today, the conversations you might have. Pray for God's kingdom (righteousness, peace and joy in the Holy Spirit) to come into all that you do today.*

"Give us this day our daily bread" *Thank God for how He meets your needs each day remembering that "every good and perfect gift is from above" (James 1:17). And then share with Him any other needs you have.*

"And forgive us of our sins as we forgive those who have sinned against us." *Remind yourself of the forgiveness that is in Christ (1 John 1:9) and think of those who you might need to forgive.*

"And lead us not to temptation but deliver us from the evil one." *Pray for God's power to help you turn from temptation and follow the life-giving ways of Jesus.*

"For thine is the kingdom, and the power, and the glory, forever and ever."

Amen

Appendix F

· ·

⟶• WHO AM I?
Identity for Those in Christ

"I am the salt of the earth." (Matthew. 5:13)

"I am the light of the world." (Matthew. 5:14)

"I am a child of God." (John 1:12)

"I am part of the true vine, a channel of Christ's life." (John 15:1, 5)

"I am Christ's friend." (John 15:15)

"I am chosen appointed by Christ to bear His fruit." (John 15:16)

"I am a slave of righteousness." (Romans 6:18)

"I am enslaved to God." (Romans 6:22)

"I am the Son of God; God is spiritually my father." (Romans 8:14,15; Galatians 3:26, 4:6)

"I am a joint heir with Christ, sharing His inheritance with Him." (Romans 8:17)

"I am a temple - a dwelling place - of God. His Spirit and His life dwells in me." (1 Corinthians 3:16, 6:19)

"I am united to the Lord and am one Spirit with Him." (1 Corinthians 6:17)

"I am a member of Christ's body." (1 Corinthians 12:27, Ephesians 5:30)

"I am a new creation." (2 Corinthians 5:17)

"I am reconciled to God and am a minister of reconciliation." (2 Corinthians 5:18,19)

"I am a son of God and one in Christ." (Galatians 3:26, 28)

"I am an heir of God since I am a son of God." (Galatians 4:6, 7)

"I am a saint." (Ephesians 1:1, 1 Corinthians. 1:2, Philippians 1:1, Colossians 1:2)

"I am God's workmanship - His handiwork - born anew in Christ to do His work." (Ephesians 2:10)

"I am a fellow citizen with the rest of God's family." (Ephesians 2:19)

"I am a prisoner of Christ." (Ephesians 3:1, 4:1)

"I am righteous and holy." (Ephesians 4:24)

"I am a citizen of heaven, seated in heaven right now." (Philippians 3:20, Ephesians 2:6)

"I am hidden with Christ in God." (Colossians 3:3)

"I am an expression of the life of Christ because He is my life." (Colossians 3:4)

"I am chosen of God, holy and dearly loved." (Colossians 3:12, 1 Thessalonians 1:4)

"I am a son of light and not of darkness." (1 Thessalonians 5:5)

"I am a holy partaker of a heavenly calling." (Hebrews 3:14)

"I am a partaker in Christ; I share in His life." (Hebrews 3:14)

"I am one of God's living stones, being built up in Christ as a spiritual house." (1 Peter 2:5)

"I am a member of a chosen race, a royal priesthood, a holy nation, a people for God's own possession." (1 Peter 2:9-10)

"I am an alien and stranger to this world in which I temporarily live." (1 Peter 2:11)

"I am a child of God and I will resemble Christ when He returns." (1 John 3:1-2)

"I am NOT the Great 'I AM' but by the grace of God, I am what I am. (Exodus 3:14, John 8:24, 28, 58, 1 Corinthians 15:10)

"Since I am in Christ, by the grace of God … I have been justified - completely forgiven and made righteous." (Romans 5:1)

"I died with Christ and died to the power of sin's rule over my life." (Romans 6:1- 6)

"I am free forever from condemnation." (Romans 8:1)

"I have been placed into Christ by God's doing." (1 Corinthians 1:30)

"I have received the Spirit of God into my life that I might know the things freely given to me by God." (1 Corinthians 2:12)

"I've been given the mind of Christ." (1 Corinthians 2:16)

"I have been bought with a price; I am not my own; I belong to God." (1 Corinthians 6:19-20)

"I have been established, anointed and sealed by God in Christ, and have been given the Holy Spirit as a pledge guaranteeing my inheritance to come." (2 Corinthians 1:21, Ephesians 1:13-14)

Appendix G

. . . .

—• **ATTRIBUTES OF GOD**

God is Jehovah. The name of independent being - I AM WHO I AM - belongs to Jehovah God. As we consider His greatness, we fall down in fear and awe of this One who possesses all authority. Exodus 3:13-15

God is Jehovah-M'Kaddesh. This name means "the God who sanctifies." A God separate from all that is evil requires that the people who follow Him be cleansed from all evil. Leviticus 20:7,8

God is Infinite. We cannot speak of measure, amount, size or weight and at the same time be speaking of God, for He is beyond measurement. God has no beginning, no end and no limits. Romans 11:33

God is Omnipotent. God has power. Since God is also infinite, whatever He has must be without limit; therefore, God has limitless power. Jeremiah 32:17-18, 26-27

God is Good. The goodness of God is what disposes Him to be kind, benevolent and full of good will toward all creation. Psalm 119:65-72

God is Love. God's love is so great that He gave His only Son to bring us into fellowship with Him. God's love not only encompasses the world but embraces each of us personally and intimately. 1 John 4:7-10

God is Jehovah-jireh. This name means "the God who provides." Just as He provided yesterday, He will provide tomorrow. He grants deliverance from sin, the oil of joy for the ashes of sorrow and eternal citizenship in His Kingdom. Genesis 22:9-14

God is Jehovah-shalom. This name means "the God of peace." God could never give to others a peace that exceeds understanding if He Himself were not perfect, unfailing peace. Judges 6:16-24

God is Immutable. All that God is, He has always been. All that He has been and is, He will ever be. He cannot change because He is perfect and will remain perfect. Psalm 102:25-28

God is Transcendent. We must not think of God as highest in an order of beings. This would be to grant Him eminence, even pre-eminence, but this is not enough. He is transcendent - existing beyond the created universe. Psalm 113:4,5

God is Just. God rules with absolute justice. Not fooled by appearances, God is fair, equitable and impartial in all of His judgments. Psalm 75:1-7

God is Holy. God's holiness is not simply the best we know made infinitely better. God is absolutely untainted. His holiness stands apart - unique and incomprehensible. Revelation 4:8-11

God is Jehovah-rophe. This name means "Jehovah heals." God alone has the remedy for the healing of mankind. The Gospel is concerned with the physical, moral and spiritual healing of all people. Exodus 15:22-26

God is Self-Sufficient. He is the One who contains all, who gives all that is given, but who Himself can receive nothing that He has not first given. Acts 17:24-28

God is Omniscient. God knows all that can be known. His knowledge includes every possible thing that exists, has ever existed or will ever exist. Psalm 139:1-6

God is Omnipresent. God is everywhere - close to everything, next to everyone. "'Do not I fill heaven and earth?' declares the Lord." Psalm 139:7-12

God is Merciful. God's compassion is infinite and inexhaustible. In the mercy of His provision in Christ, He took upon Himself the judgment that was due us. He waits and works now for all people everywhere to turn to Him, not wanting any to be lost. Deuteronomy 4:29-31

God is Sovereign. God is in control of our lives. His sovereignty is the attribute by which He rules His entire creation. To be sovereign, God must be all-knowing and all-powerful. 1 Chronicles 29:11-13

God is Jehovah-nissi. This name means "God our banner." We may go from triumph to triumph and say, "Thanks be to God, who gives us the victory through our Lord Jesus Christ" (1 Corinthians 15:57). Exodus 17:8-15

God is Wise. All God's acts are done in infinite wisdom. He always acts for our good, which is to conform us to Christ. Our good and His glory are inextricably bound together. Proverbs 3:19-20

God is Faithful. Our hope for the future rests upon God's faithfulness. Because He is faithful, His covenants will stand and His promises will be honored. Psalm 89:1-8

God is Wrathful. God's wrath is never capricious, self-indulgent or irritable, as human anger often is. Instead, it is a right and necessary reaction to objective moral evil. Nahum 1:2-8

God is full of Grace. Grace is the good pleasure of God that inclines Him to grant merit where it is undeserved and to forgive debt that cannot be repaid. Ephesians 1:5-8

God is our Comforter. Jesus called the Holy Spirit the "Comforter." Paul writes that the Lord is "the God of all comfort." 2 Corinthians 1:3-4

God is El-Shaddai. This name means "God Almighty." It is best understood as God who is all-sufficient and all-bountiful - the source of all blessings, fullness and fruitfulness. Genesis 49:22-26

God is Father. The Creator of the universe cares for each one of us as if we are the only child He has. Jesus taught us to pray, "Our Father" (Matthew 6:9). The Spirit of God taught us to cry, "Abba, Father," as in the intimacy of the family. Romans 8:15-17

God is the Church's head. God the Son, Jesus, is the head of the Church. The head - as the part of the body that sees, hears, thinks and decides - gives the orders that the rest of the body lives by. Ephesians 1:22-23

God is our Intercessor. Knowing our temptations, God the Son intercedes for us. He opens the doors for us to boldly ask Him for mercy. Thus, God is both the starting point and ending point of true prayer. Hebrews 4:14-16

God is Adonai. This name means "Master" or "Lord." God as Adonai calls all God's people to acknowledge themselves as His servants, recognizing His right to command them as the Lord of their lives. 2 Samuel 7:18-20

God is Elohim. This name means "Strength" or "Power." He is transcendent, mighty and strong. Elohim is the great name of God, signifying supreme power, sovereignty and a covenant relationship that He is ever faithful to keep. Genesis 17:7-8

Navigators 2007

Appendix H

. . . .

⟶● THE IMMANUEL MOMENT
Adapted from Rev. Kathleen Christopher and Dr. Karl D. Lehman

―――――

"Prayer is above all listening to the voice of Jesus, who dwells in the depths of the heart. Jesus does not force himself on us; his voice is reserved. Whatever we may do in our lives, let us never fail to listen to the voice of the Lord in our hearts. Because in our restless, noisy world the loving voice of God is easily drowned out." - Henri Nouwen.

―――――

Imagine you are sitting on a rock next to a gurgling mountain stream. It's spring, so the leaves on the trees rising all around you glow bright green in the sunlight. Feel the mountain air on your face; it's fresh, but not cold. Now imagine Jesus takes a seat next to you. What if He has something He would like to say to you? And what would you like to say to Him? Ask Him?

If prayer is, as Nouwen says, "listening to the voice of Jesus," then the Immanuel Moment is a way to allow the Holy Spirit to use the eyes of our heart (our imaginations and memories) to create a space, perhaps like the scene above, where we can actively listen to Him and even interact with Him.

We can do this because of two realities:

- Jesus lives in us, nearer to us than our own breath (John 14:20). He is "with us always, to the end of the age" (Matthew 28:20). This is the meaning of the name Immanuel, God with us (Matthew 1:23).

- God created us so that expressions of gratitude and appreciation warm and enliven our neural pathways, preparing us for connection. God says we gain access to Him through thanksgiving: "Enter his gates with thanksgiving, and his courts with praise! Give thanks to him; bless his name" (Psalm 100:4).

Putting these realities together, we can use the Immanuel Moment exercise to intentionally engage in deep and personal expressions of gratitude and appreciation to God, preparing ourselves to connect with Him. And then we can ask Him to allow us to perceive His presence and hear His voice. The goal is to establish an interactive intimacy with God that carries on into our everyday lives. Use this exercise as often as you like. It can also be useful and powerful to do this exercise together with a prayer partner or small group.

Immanuel Moment Exercise

1. Open in prayer.

"Lord, thank you that you are always with me. I consecrate myself to you today and give you access to every part of me. Please prepare my mind and heart to hear Your voice and to know and love you as you truly are. Please be Lord over all my thoughts, memories and emotions. Please bind and silence my spiritual enemies by the power of your name. Please also quiet the voice of my flesh. I ask you to sanctify and enliven the eyes of my heart - my imagination - for your purposes. I put my trust in you, the great shepherd and lover of my soul, and ask you to create a safe place for me to experience your presence with me. In your holy name, Amen."

2. Quiet your heart and body.

Make yourself comfortable. Breathe deeply in and out. Notice any areas of your body that are tense. Relax.

3. Express your gratitude and appreciation.

Ask the Lord to take you either in your memory or your imagination to:

- a time when you felt especially close or connected to Him; *or*
- a time or place where you felt especially grateful; *or*
- a place He will create and give you to meet with Him.

From that place in your memory or imagination, express your gratitude and appreciation to God. Thank Him for everything you can think of to thank Him for. Bless Him with any words you can think in appreciation of who He is. Do this for at least three minutes.

4. Ask the Lord to allow you to be aware of His presence.

If, in this place of thanksgiving, you are not yet aware of the living presence of the Lord, ask Him if He would allow you to receive His presence with you.

5. If you are aware of His presence, ask Him if there is anything He would like to show you or say to you. Listen carefully.

Note: Whatever we believe we hear from the Lord must be consistent with Scripture and should also resonate with our mature Christian friends or mentors.

6. Ask Him anything you would like to know.

7. If you cannot perceive Him, ask Him if He will show you if anything is in the way. Respond accordingly.

Appendix I

. . . .

➔• THE ROLE OF HEALING PRAYER IN DISCIPLESHIP

Jesus compressed His whole teaching into two rules: He wants us to love God with all our heart, soul, mind and strength and to love our neighbor as ourselves (Matthew 22:37-39).

A disciple of Jesus, then, is a person in the process of allowing Jesus to shape them into a great lover of God and of others. John, one of the first disciples of Jesus, said we can only do this - love God and others - when we know and trust that God loves us first (1 John 4:16, 19). God's love for us is the fuel for our loving Him and others.

As simple as this sounds, if you have followed Jesus for any amount of time you must have discovered that knowing God loves you - truly, joyfully, loves you - and loving God back and loving your neighbor proves anything but easy. This is because sin, wounds and warfare obstruct our hearts. God's love doesn't flow in, and our love doesn't flow out.

So as we walk the path of discipleship we will at various times realize we are stuck. We can't get past a barrier to receiving God's love, loving God or loving someone else. We may need intensive healing prayer to help us get "unstuck."

The goal of the Intensive Healing Prayer (IHP) team at Greenwood is to create a safe space for followers of Jesus to experience a deep, personal encounter with Him so He can restore our souls (Psalm 23:3); healing us from of the impact of sin, wounds and warfare; and thereby freeing us to receive God's love so we can love Him and others.

———

John Eldredge says this about healing prayer: *"This is the most beautiful form of prayer - prayer for the healing of the heart and soul. At its very best, all prayer is deep communion, drawing us into intimacy and union with our God. When that intimacy and union reaches the damaged places with us, it is like the spring showers that come to Death Valley - wildflowers burst forth from barren ground, and the land looks like Eden again. The inner healing that occurs is more beautiful than anything in nature that has taken your breath away. For the heart and soul of a human being is worth far more than all the beautiful places in the world." Moving Mountains*

———

If you choose to seek IHP at Greenwood, you will meet with a team of two or three trained prayer ministers several times for prayer sessions lasting between 1 ½ to 2 hours. The team will not 'counsel' you. They will attempt to facilitate and support your personal interaction with Jesus, trusting that Jesus Himself will direct the prayer time, moving gently and lovingly through the damaged places of your soul to bring healing. He may want to help you recover from generational sin, unhealed memories, demonic oppression, lies, guilt, unforgiveness or anger at God.

For more information about IHP, contact Jasona Brown at JBrown@GeenwoodCC.com.

Appendix J

· ·

⟶● PRAYER, CARE AND SHARE

Sharing the gospel can often feel very intimidating. Maybe we fear we won't have all the answers, or we don't want to offend someone. The honest reality is that it is hard. Our secular, humanistic culture is generally apathetic, spiritually jaded and relativistic. People don't care, or their guard goes up when you start talking about spiritual things; or they relegate spiritual matters to ones' individual feelings. The 21st Century Motto is "You do You." Considering these realities, it can feel almost impossible to share the gospel with others.

We need to remember that in the time of Jesus and during the early church, the world was also pretty messed up. In fact, even worse than today. Many historians would say it was a world of suffering, fear, inequality and racism as seen by slavery, plagues, infanticide and constant war. And yet, God said, "All authority in heaven and earth has been given to me. Therefore go!" And the early church went with the power and hope of the gospel to rescue and restore our lost and broken world. And the miraculous happened. A marginalized and persecuted rag-tag group of followers of Jesus - called 'The Way' - slowly changed the Roman world with the ways of Jesus.

We too have been called to "Go"!

We use the 'Prayer, Care, Share' model to encourage you in sharing the gospel. Read through the following explanation and cut out the bookmark. Prayerfully select a couple of people (maybe a friend, family member, co-worker or neighbor) to pray for, care for and share with.

Our first step is not "working up" the passion and utilizing the latest witnessing tools. The first step is for our hearts to break; that we would be like God who grieves over the destructive wake of sin and longs for His people to return to Him! So the best way to start is in prayer; praying for our hearts and praying for others. As we pray for others, our hearts will slowly awaken and align more to God's heart for them.

PRAYER
Align with Jesus in Prayer

- Father, draw _____ to your Son Jesus, give them holy desires for you and quench their thirst with Jesus (John 4:10-14, 7:37-40).
- Show _____ the deceitful, destructive, enslaving power of their sin and free them in Jesus (Romans 6:15-18).
- Open their hearts to see King Jesus as the greatest treasure they can possess and give them the joy of repentance (Matthew 13:44-46, Acts 3:19).

CARE
Radically love and serve people
- Who is a person in need that you can care for?
- How could you be caring for them in a way that reflects a radical love?

SHARE
Speak the gospel in an engaging and transformative way
- Listen to the Holy Spirit about what aspect of the Gospel will connect best with their story and greatest angst (desire/longing, enslavement/ addiction, forgiveness/cleansing).
- What part of the gospel in your story might connect with their story?
- Key gospel ideas and scriptures (memorize these verses):

God's Love:
"For God so loved the world, that he gave his only son, that whoever believes in him should not perish but have eternal life." John 3:16

"But God demonstrates his own love for us in this: While we were still sinners, Christ died for us." Romans 5:8

The Problem:
"For all have sinned and fall short of the glory of God." Romans 3:23

The Solution:
"For the wages of sin is death, but the gift of God is eternal life in Christ Jesus our Lord." Romans 6:23

"That if you confess with your mouth, 'Jesus is Lord,' and believe in your heart that God raised him from the dead, you will be saved." Romans 10:9-10

PRAYER · CARE · SHARE
A Holy-Spirit-led, grace-infilled, life-changing journey.

Psalm 96:1-4
Sing to the Lord a new song;
sing to the Lord, all the earth.
Sing to the Lord, praise his name;
proclaim his salvation day after day.
Declare his glory among the nations,
his marvelous deeds among all peoples.

For great is the Lord and most worthy of praise; he is to be feared above all gods.

Prayer

_____

_____

Care

_____

Share

_____

Appendix K

. . . .

—• THE REMAINING TASK OF MISSIONS

God's mission flows from God's heart to our lost and broken world. Jesus' last command to the disciples before He ascended into heaven was, "You will receive power when the Holy Spirit comes on you; and you will be my witnesses in Jerusalem, and in all Judea and Samaria, and to the ends of the earth" (Acts 1:8). God desires for all to be saved (1 Timothy 2:4) and that includes going to the ends of the earth to share the hope, love and salvation of Jesus to every ethnic group (Matthew 28:19). This is not a burden for us to carry but rather a sacred mission to be a part of.

The Remaining Task
For more information on the remaining task, see joshuaproject.net.

"Frontier People Groups (FPGs) are Unreached People Groups with 0.1% or fewer Christians of any kind, and no evidence of a self-sustaining gospel movement. There are about 4,761 Frontier People Groups with a total population of 1,820,899,000. One-fourth of the world lives in FPGs and have almost no chance of hearing about Jesus from someone in their own people group." JoshuaProject.net/frontier

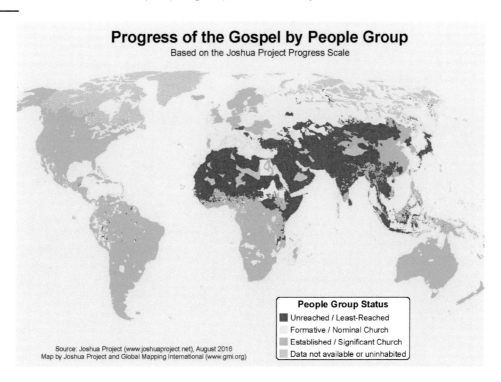

Progress of the Gospel by People Group
Based on the Joshua Project Progress Scale

People Group Status
- Unreached / Least-Reached
- Formative / Nominal Church
- Established / Significant Church
- Data not available or uninhabited

Source: Joshua Project (www.joshuaproject.net), August 2016
Map by Joshua Project and Global Mapping International (www.gmi.org)

⟶ 6 WAYS TO REACH GOD'S WORLD

LEARN. PRAY. GO. SEND. WELCOME. MOBILIZE.
(From https://omf.org/us/6-ways/)

Learn
- Read a missionary biography (*Hudson Taylor's Spiritual Secret, Bruchko;
  A Chance to Die; The Life and Legacy of Amy Carmichael*).
- Take a course like *Perspectives* on the *World Christian Movement.*
- Read about unreached people groups at JoshuaProject.net.

Pray
- Sign up for prayer letters from the mission partners of your church.
- Purchase the *Operation World* book and pray for people in a different country each day.
- Join or start a prayer group through your church to pray for missionaries and
  unreached people groups.

Go
- Go on a short-term cross-cultural trip with your church.
- Use your profession to share the hope and love of Christ among the nations.
- Commit to serve long-term overseas.

Send
- Financially support a missionary or project.
- Encourage a missionary via care packages, email or social media.
- Welcome missionaries home in practical ways by preparing a meal, lending
  a car or a guest room.

Welcome
- Become a friendship partner with an International Student Ministry
  (i.e. International Students Inc.).
- Volunteer with a refugee ministry (i.e., Restoration Outreach Programs).
- Introduce yourself to internationals in your neighborhood, place of work or
  at a grocery store.

Mobilize
- Volunteer with a mission organization.
- Advocate for a people group or a cause.
- Invite a friend to join you on a short-term mission trip.

RESOURCES

Videos

- *Prayercast Nation Videos (prayercast.com)*
- *Tears of the Saints* (YouTube)
- *Never the Same, Celebrating 50 Years since Peace Child* (YouTube)
- *Six Ways to Reach God's World* (YouTube)

Leader's Guide

....

On a hot summer day, when you were a kid at the local swimming pool, did you ever climb the ladder to the high dive and leap off into the cool refreshing water? If it was your first time, there was probably much trepidation and you might have even climbed back down again. This Discipleship Guide is like a diving board into the pool of a deeper, life-giving relationship with Jesus and others. The point is not the diving board, the point is to experience the pool. Likewise, the point is not the Discipleship Guide, rather, it enables us to be formed more like Christ through life-on-life discipleship. And you might have some fears and trepidations, but don't worry, God is not looking for perfect people. He is looking for willing people to take the leap with Him.

Without the guidance and transformative power of the Holy Spirit, this discipleship process is totally empty. We need to invite God into this process by **PRIORITIZING PRAYER**! First, go before God and acknowledge where your heart is. Do you have any worries or fears? Any misconceptions about discipleship? Any pride that you need to confess? Then pray for the individuals that will be in your group. Ask for God's sensitivity, wisdom and boldness to see more of their hearts and their barriers to intimacy with Him. Pray that God will open their eyes to see more of Jesus and His ways for us. During the process of leading people through the Discipleship Guide, take 20 minutes once a week to go for a walk and pray for them. Possibly send them a text message of encouragement.

· Before you start leading a group or an individual through the Discipleship Guide, please read through the 'Opening Concepts' to understand the heart, vision and direction of the guide. It is not necessary to go through the whole guide beforehand but skim over it to get an overall feel.

· The Discipleship Guide is organized into 12 sessions with a focus on the 9 'Invitations of Jesus.' You can choose to meet every week, bi-weekly or monthly. We encourage frequency and consistency to build on the conversation and relationships. If you do not finish a lesson or discern that you need to spend more time on a particular topic, please don't rush through. Listen to the Holy Spirit's guidance.

· Encourage everyone to study the sessions before you meet. This will help them go to a greater depth of engagement and interaction with others in the group. As you personally prepare to lead the lesson, take the time to go through the material and allow the Spirit of God to speak directly to you. A Study Bible might be a helpful resource to understand some of the deeper intricacies of Scripture. We suggest the NIV Study Bible or the ESV Study Bible.

- If you are in a Small Group context where there are more than eight people, we encourage you to break up into smaller groups if possible. If you are in a co-ed group, it might be very helpful to divide into groups of men or women. If you discern the need to follow up with someone individually, please consider getting together with them one-on-one.

- As you lead the discussion and facilitate the time, remember that this is not a time to "teach" or give a "lecture." You are facilitating a head, heart and hands engagement. Like Jesus' model of ministry, ask questions. Use the Discipleship Guide to ask questions and ask further questions as the Spirit leads. Help them to discover the truth for themselves. Ask other group members what they think. There may be times you need to give a greater explanation, and that is okay. Prioritize the conversation and self-discovery.

- If someone asks you a question and you do not have an answer, be honest and say, "That is a great question, and I don't have an answer for you right now. I'll look into it. Does anyone else have some thoughts on that question?"

- Don't be afraid of silence. People often need time to think about the question. Typically, it is helpful to count for seven seconds in your head to wait for an answer or follow up with a different question.

- While you are discipling someone, you might discover an unrepentant sin issue. Don't freak out! First off, remember your "plank eye." As Jesus said, "First take the plank out of your own eye, and then you will see clearly to remove the speck from your brother and sister's eye" (Matthew 7:5). So, pray first and acknowledge your own sin and approach their sin with a posture of grace and truth. If they do not listen to you, follow the biblical model of inviting others into the situation (Matthew 18:15-17). Please feel free to contact any of the pastors or elders for help.

- The Discipleship Guide sessions are broken up into categories of Story, Study, Scripture, Head/Heart/Hands questions, Spiritual Exercise, Lectio Divina and Memory Verse. There is a lot of material and it can feel daunting. Let the Spirit guide you on how to use it and where to focus. Remember that the Discipleship Guide is a tool for life-on-life discipleship.

  » We suggest you read the story together and then ask, "How does this story resonate with you? Any thoughts?"
  » Then read through the Scripture sections and the corresponding Head, Heart and Hands questions. There may be times it would be appropriate to deviate from the question. Maybe somebody already raised the question, or a better question was asked. Feel free to add any appropriate questions that might help to get to the heart of the thought.

- » For the Spiritual Exercise section, ask them if they have done it and what their experience was. If they have not, encourage them to do so.
- » For the Lectio Divina section, use Appendix A to guide you. This is an incredibly important opportunity for them to personally hear God's voice through Scripture and to experience the Word of God as "living and active, sharper than any double-edged sword, it penetrates even to dividing soul and spirit, joints and marrow; it judges the thoughts and attitudes of the heart" (Hebrews 4:12).
- » And finally, there is a memory verse. It might feel like it is only kids in Sunday School who memorize Bible verses. But as Jesus said when he was being tempted by Satan, quoting a verse He memorized from Deuteronomy, "Man does not live on bread alone, but on every word that comes from the mouth of God" (Matthew 4:4). So we too need to memorize, meditate and store God's word in our minds and hearts as the life-giving Word it is.

- Periodically summarize the ideas and thoughts from the session. This helps give clarity and continuity to the lesson. But don't preach.

We hope and pray that as you disciple someone using the Discipleship Guide, you will experience the sweet joy of God powerfully and beautifully at work. And that both of you would leap off the high dive into the cool, refreshing water, experiencing a deeper life-giving relationship with God and others.

Recommended Reading List of the Authors

. . . .

Kay's Recommendations:
1. *The God of All Comfort* by Hannah Whitall Smith
2. *The Knowledge of the Holy* by A.W. Tozer
3. *Invitation to Retreat* by Ruth Haley Barton
4. *The Life You've Always Wanted* by John Ortberg
5. *The Freedom of Self-Forgetfulness* by Timothy Keller
6. *Deep Unto Deep* by Dana Candler

Adam's Recommendations:
1. *Disappointment with God* by Philip Yancey
2. *The Prodigal God* by Timothy Keller
3. *Eternity in their Hearts* by Don Richardson
4. *Truth & Transformation* - A Manifesto for Ailing Nations by Vishal Mangalwadi
5. *Wild at Heart* by John Eldredge
6. *The Jesus Storybook Bible* by Sally Lloyd-Jones

Doug's recommendations
1. *Stone by Stone - Tearing Down the Wall Between God's Heart and Yours* by Jasona Brown
2. *The Pursuit of God* by A.W. Tozer
3. *The Sacred Romance* by John Eldredge
4. *Waking the Dead* by John Eldredge
5. *Eternity is Now in Session* by John Ortberg
6. *The Healing Presence* by Leanne Payne

Made in the USA
San Bernardino, CA
12 November 2019